Culture and Conflict in Global Perspective

Bertelsmann Stiftung (ed.)

Culture and Conflict in Global Perspective

The Cultural Dimensions of Conflicts
from 1945 to 2007

Aurel Croissant
Uwe Wagschal
Nicolas Schwank
Christoph Trinn

| **Verlag** Bertelsmann**Stiftung**

Bibliographic information published by the Deutsche Nationalbibliothek

The Deutsche Nationalbibliothek lists this publication in the
Deutsche Nationalbibliografie; detailed bibliographic data
is available on the Internet at http://dnb.d-nb.de.

© 2010 Verlag Bertelsmann Stiftung, Gütersloh
Executive Editor: Malte C. Boecker, Leila Ulama-Benazzouz
Copy Editor: Heike Herrberg
Production Editor: Christiane Raffel
Cover Design: Nadine Humann
Cover Illustration: "The Islamic Project (Witnesses of the Future)"
AES artists group, © VG Bild-Kunst, Bonn 2009
Typesetting and Printing: Hans Kock Buch- und Offsetdruck GmbH, Bielefeld
ISBN 978-3-86793-058-1

www.bertelsmann-stiftung.org/publications

Contents

Preface

As the world grows smaller, its religions and cultures are interacting with each other to a greater degree than ever before in human history. Over the past years, my husband and I have therefore taken a great interest in the topic of cultural orientation as well as in the issue of how people of different cultural backgrounds can live together in peace. Ultimately, the questions these topics raise are: What holds society together when it is home to diverse cultural and religious elements? How can culture promote understanding among disparate social subgroups or between entire countries? What are the changes we face as technological progress continues to alter our already globalized world? And how can people of different cultures and religions come together in peace?

In recent years, the Bertelsmann Stiftung has addressed these issues through its International Cultural Dialogue series and its Religion Monitor, among other efforts. Discussions with public figures around the world held as part of these projects have made clear that culture can play dual roles: It can serve as an enriching, civilizing force that facilitates spiritual growth within the global community, and it can simultaneously serve as an inflammatory factor that fuels conflicts and crises.

Each year, conjointly with the Salzburg Festival, the Salzburg Trialogue brings together international political, business and cultural leaders to discuss the most-pressing issues confronting Europe and the world. The international experts present at the 2007 Salzburg Trialogue noted with regret that the commonalities of the globe's diverse religions and cultures are often emphasized in a way that makes their differences seem superficial or insignificant. In times of conflict, unfortunately, we discover that this is not how things truly are. Seemingly trivial happenings can turn into explosive events, and what appears to outsiders as a minor issue can have a major emotional impact on those directly affected by it. People who have coexisted peacefully for years suddenly find themselves at odds with each other, and former friends become enemies. The violent conflicts that ensue from such situations are a source of great suffering for humanity. Since the advent of globalization, moreover, many people have become afraid that their own culture will soon disappear and that they will end up "culturally homeless" as a result.

Those developments are what have given rise to this study, which is meant to shed light on the role that culture plays in the globe's conflicts. Through the study, we would like to make it possible to take a more nuanced look at how the interaction of the world's various cultures influences whether we experience conflict or peace. It is also meant to encourage people everywhere to increase their efforts to promote peace by identifying even more effective approaches to intercultural dialogue. Ultimately, I am convinced that, by emphasizing tolerance and understanding, all of the world's inhabitants can live together in peace.

Liz Mohn
Vice Chairwoman, Bertelsmann Stiftung

Foreword

This study on the role of culture in conflicts of global importance is the result of extensive collaboration between the Institute of Political Science at the University of Heidelberg and the Bertelsmann Stiftung. A number of events informed our mutual desire to objectify, through the use of comprehensive data, the often highly emotional debate on how the world's diverse cultures can—and cannot—coexist.

Reports of conflicts with a cultural background have proliferated recently, not just in the media, but also in the *Conflict Barometer*, published at the University of Heidelberg to assess global strife. Of this, the global uproar in 2006 over the Danish cartoons of the Prophet Mohammed is just one high-profile example. Along with this trend, the desire grew to carry out a systematic assessment of the world's conflicts. In addition, during the activities organized as part of the Bertelsmann Stiftung's International Cultural Dialogue series, it became increasingly clear that there was a growing need around the globe for concrete strategies to address cultural conflicts. Yet, in order to know where strategies for promoting intercultural dialogue might prove most effective, it is also imperative to know how cultural differences give rise to and fuel conflicts.

In addition, both the Bertelsmann Stiftung and the Institute of Political Science wanted to contribute to the European Year of Intercultural Dialogue in 2008 by engaging in a differentiated examination of the "clash of civilizations," as formulated by the political scientist Samuel Huntington.

Those were the circumstances that ultimately gave rise to the following questions, which this study aims to address: What are the core characteristics of cultural conflict? How can such conflicts be categorized? Is culturally fed strife becoming more dominant within the world's various conflicts? To what extent do cultural factors influence the genesis and progression of conflicts? Given empirical findings, how should actors dedicated to cultural dialogue react? The team of researchers led by Prof. Aurel Croissant and Prof. Uwe Wagschal has prepared this study with the utmost care. With regard to methodology, they have taken a major, pioneering step with their definition and operationalization of cultural conflict. In particular, their focus on religion, language and historicity as identity-giving cultural factors has proven especially insightful.

Above all, our findings give rise to a key realization: Although cultural conflicts have increased significantly, neither a purported "clash of civilizations" nor religious differences can be seen as the key drivers of international tensions. For the most part, political conflicts result from a confluence of factors. Yet, as soon as cultural issues enter into political strife, the chances increase that violence will ensue. For that reason, this study's essential message is that cultural conflicts must be analyzed in a differentiated manner in order to recognize and reduce the threat early on of cultural aspects being instrumentalized to aggravate political differences. The most important strategies to this end are the promotion of intercultural dialogue and the improvement of basic sociopolitical conditions. Cultural conditioning might be a given—to make use of a thesis advanced by Lee Kuan Yew, former prime minister of Singapore—but cultural conflicts are not.

The Bertelsmann Stiftung would like to thank all of those who helped produce this study, first and foremost the authors and the academic specialists at the University of Heidelberg, for their fruitful collaboration, as well as the employees of the Bertelsmann Stiftung. In addition, we would like to thank all of the experts who participated in this study's development phase or who were involved in presenting the initial findings in Heidelberg and at the International Cultural Forum in Vietnam. They include Prof. Helmut Anheier, Dr. Matthias Basedau, Prof. Thorsten Bonacker, Prof. Sven Chojnacki, Prof. Ulrich Eith, Dr. Gero Erdmann, Prof. Johan Galtung, Prof. Hans Gebhard, Prof. Andreas Hasenclever, Josef Janning, Prof. Hans Keman, Dr. Patrick Köllner, Prof. Gudrun Krämer, Prof. Jan-Erik Lane, Prof. Surendra Munshi, Prof. Dieter Senghaas and Dr. Peter Thiery.

Malte C. Boecker, LL.M.
Senior Expert, Bertelsmann Stiftung

Introduction

Over the past two decades, the relationship between culture and conflict has been the subject of controversy among both academic specialists and the public alike. A key factor shaping attitudes in the West, at least for a period of time, was the "clash of civilizations" envisioned by Samuel Huntington in 1993. While other researchers (Fukuyama 1992) foresaw "the end of history" following the collapse of the Soviet Union, Huntington was convinced that culture would become the driving force behind future international tensions. He was particularly concerned about the conflictual fault lines running between the Western and the Islamic world.

Now, more than 15 years later, Huntington's thesis has been subjected to extensive scrutiny by social scientists, and a clash of civilizations, as he originally described it, is not to be found either on the international policy level or among nation-states—that, at least, is the almost unanimous opinion among experts today.

At the same time, it is apparent that his paradigm remains stubbornly part of the media's reportage and that, in the major international conflicts after 1990 between the United States and Afghanistan and the United States and Iraq, those states were involved that, according to Huntington, serve as important representatives of their "civilizations." In the conflict in 2006 surrounding the cartoons published in Denmark depicting the Prophet Mohammed, hundreds of thousands of people took to the streets to demonstrate—in some cases, violently—against what they perceived to be an insult to Islam. Similar if less strident reactions were evident following the speech given by Pope Benedict XVI at the University of Regensburg in September 2006.

Even more readily than on the international or transnational levels, examples can be found within individual states of conflicts in which opposing values and identities seem to play a dominant role. Such "cultural" conflicts—sometimes less precisely described as "ethnic," "ethno-religious" or "ethno-national"—are hardly new. What's more, they are not to be found only in "Islamic" countries or countries home to Muslim populations. Religion, language and varying interpretations of "historical identity" serve to fuel disputes in many countries and regions with highly diverse cultural pasts, disputes that often involve violence. A few better-known examples include the religious conflict in Northern Ireland between Protestants and Catholics, the linguistic conflict relating to French-speaking Canada, the historicitary conflict—that is, the dispute focusing on heritage and history—between Hutus and Tutsis in Rwanda, and the linguistic and religious conflict between Tamils and Singhalese in Sri Lanka.

Consequently, the social-scientific literature offers myriad studies on how such conflicts arise and progress and the consequences thereof. This study, however, can be seen as a new empirical contribution to assessing the importance of culture; in addition, it focuses on cultural factors in conflicts all across the globe. In summary form, it presents the results of a much more comprehensive investigation carried out by the authors on behalf of the Bertelsmann Stiftung at the University of Heidelberg's Institute of Political Science over the past year (Croissant et al. 2009).

The extended study, the summary and a special report on Asia (Croissant and Trinn 2009) all focus squarely on the concept of "cultural conflicts." As a result of a lengthy discourse that took place on the diverse approaches favored by researchers in the social sciences, which can only be briefly outlined here, cultural conflicts have been defined as follows: domestic, interstate or transnational political conflicts, in which participating actors make reference to language, religion and/or historical contexts (hereafter referred to as "historicity").

14

It must be emphasized that cultural conflicts are defined by the subject of the conflict and not, as is often the case, by the underlying "causes," in the sense of effecting agents. That means that cultural conflicts do not necessarily ensue from cultural differences (e.g., as language or religion) between social groups.

Cultural conflicts are political conflicts in which culture serves as the conflict issue. In designating a conflict as "cultural," the focus is thus not on the causes of the conflict or the motives of the actors but, rather, on the issues that the actors refer to over the course of the conflict through their statements or actions and the meaning they assign to them. Accordingly, in a cultural conflict, cultural factors such as religious or "ethnic" differences are not necessarily the cause of the conflict.

The conceptualization of cultural conflicts and the differentiation of culture as a social phenomenon according to the dimensions of language, religion and historicity (see Chapter 2 for concept definitions) make it possible to distinguish cultural from non-cultural conflicts. In addition, this allows cultural conflicts to be differentiated into a number of types. As can be seen in the following discussion, such differentiation is highly productive when subjecting global conflicts to empirical analysis.

This study was designed with the following three objectives in mind: First, it was meant to examine the provenance of cultural conflicts and provide a theoretically well-founded definition for them, in particular, by contrasting them to other conflict types.

Second, the study was designed to examine conflicts around the world in the period from 1945 to 2007. The empiric foundations were supplied through the CONIS (Conflict Information System) dataset developed at the Institute of Political Science, which combines the advantages of a qualitative definition of conflict with those of a quantitative analysis. The dataset was particularly suitable for the undertaking at hand given its precise definition, the scope of the available data and the differentiation of conflicts into different levels of intensity, from a lack of violence to full-fledged warfare.

Third, the study was meant to examine whether and to what extent cultural factors could explain the appearance and progress of both political disputes, in general, and cultural conflicts, in particular. Such a discussion implied the need for a shift in perspective. While the descriptive-empirical approach to cultural conflicts inquires into their forms, frequencies and distributions, the focus now shifts to the explanatory power of culture as one of numerous possible causes of conflict.

The results of the empirical-descriptive approach, meaning those answering to the first two objectives, give rise to five conclusions:
- Cultural conflicts, meaning conflicts in which culture is the issue at hand, constitute a considerable share of the globe's overall conflicts. Since the mid-1980s, the total number of cultural conflicts (i.e., the sum of all forms of cultural conflict around the globe) has exceeded the number of non-cultural conflicts. In 2007, the number was higher than it had ever been in the past.
- In the vast majority of cases, cultural conflicts are a domestic phenomenon, with more than four-fifths taking place within the borders of individual nation-states. Cultural disputes between states—that form of "cultural collision" that Huntington depicted in exaggerated form as the key difficulty plaguing international relations at the end of the 20th century—are, from a numerical point of view, the exception and not the rule.
- Cultural conflicts take place, both within and between states, above all in the form of religious and historicitary disputes. Thus, the end of the Cold War represents a break in the development of cultural conflicts, something that is particularly true for religious and historicitary conflicts on the domestic level. Their number has grown considerably since the fall of the Iron Curtain.

- On both the domestic and interstate levels, cultural conflicts are particularly prone to violence. While the number of non-cultural conflicts declines when the conflict levels increase, the reverse is true for cultural conflicts, meaning that the higher the level of violence, the more cultural conflicts are present.
- Findings on global conflicts must be differentiated according to geography, with domestic conflicts exhibiting considerable regional differences. Religious conflicts, for example, are typical in the Middle East. In Asia, the spectrum of cultural conflicts is dominated by historicitary conflicts, while Europe tends toward linguistic conflicts. Conflicts in North and South America (referred to here simply as "the Americas") are clearly characterized by non-cultural aspects. Only Africa lacks a predominant trend.

Looking at this study's third objective—examining culture as an explanatory factor for conflict—five main findings present themselves:
- First and foremost, cultural structures are significant factors in explaining the appearance of conflict, something that holds true for both cultural and non-cultural conflicts. One of the study's key findings is that, as a society experiences increasing cultural fragmentation—especially linguistic fragmentation—the probability of domestic cultural conflict increases, as does the probability of interstate conflict.
- In terms of which cultural variable plays a predominant role, the research shows that language is a key cause, even more so than religious fragmentation, and that linguistic fragmentation significantly increases the probability of conflict both within and between states.
- Cultural factors are not omnipotent "master variables," that is, ones that are capable of explaining conflicts on their own. Since conflicts are complex in nature, they are better explained by several factors working in concert. Non-cultural factors, for example, are sometimes even more telling than cultural ones, in particular, the "youth bulge" used to describe the high share of young men in a given population.

- When they interact with other, non-cultural factors, cultural conflicts can increase in potency. Above all, the combination of cultural fragmentation and youth bulge is often a key driver of domestic conflicts.
- The final finding has much to say about the assumption, which is often advanced in the relevant literature, of a linear causality between religious fragmentation and conflict, meaning that the probability of conflict increases in a given society the more heterogeneous its religious structures are. Our study suggests a non-linear relationship between religious diversity and social conflict. This means that countries which are either extremely fragmented or highly homogenous are less subject to strife than countries with a moderate level of religious fragmentation.

The following chapter details the study's theoretical and definitional foundations. In a second step, an empirical topography of the various forms of cultural conflict is presented and illustrated using select examples. Four conflicts are used to represent the diverse types of conflict: the historicitary conflict in Indonesia's Aceh region, the linguistic conflict in Belgium, the religious conflict in Nigeria and the transnational conflict resulting from the 2005 publication of the Mohammed cartoons in Denmark. Thereafter, the causes of cultural conflict are analyzed, and the ability of specific cultural factors to explain conflict is examined. Finally, the study's findings are discussed in light of their real-world political implications.

Cultural Conflicts

A first objective of this study is to provide a theoretically well-founded definition of cultural conflict and to differentiate this concept from other thematic types of conflict.

Cultural conflicts as conflicts referencing culture

Cultural conflicts are one among several forms of political conflict.

> Political conflicts are understood here as controversies between two or more actors over at least one conflict issue that are carried out by measurable means.

The "political" in political conflicts results from an interaction of the concepts of "state," "security" and "highest-level social norms." That is, political conflicts always refer to the state, either through the involvement of a state or when the nation-state's most basic concern, ensuring security, is affected. This is the case when, within a given territory, physical security diminishes, regardless of whether this actually happens, is perceived to happen or might potentially happen. The threat of diminishing security is always present when a party to a conflict claims that a highest-level social norm (e.g., constitutional law, international law or human rights) has been violated and when this accusation is not addressed within the framework of the relevant norm (e.g., before a national or international court of law recognized as legitimate by the affected party).

Ultimately, a conflict is nothing other than a "communication situation" (Gurr 1970: 223 ff.): The parties to the conflict are partners in communication, the conflict activities are the means of communication (media) and the conflict issue is the communication content (subject). Not only linguistic statements, but every instance of action (e.g., a terrorist attack) can be considered as means of communication.

As a form of communication, political conflict is always located within a structurally conceived sociocultural context. This context standardizes communication since it increases the probability of certain issues arising and certain media being used at certain times by certain actors, as compared to conceivable alternatives (Krallmann and Ziemann 2001: 249; Hansen 2000: 39; Billington et al. 1991: 5). The sociocultural context can be broken down into the social context (e.g., political institutions and economic and demographic structures) and the cultural context (i.e., culture).

In general, political conflicts can be grouped into three categories:
- Conflicts between non-state actors within a nation-state or between a nation-state and a non-state actor seen as belonging to it (*domestic conflicts*)
- Conflicts between nation-states (*interstate conflicts*)
- Conflicts between non-state actors of different national backgrounds or between a nation-state and non-state actors associated with another state (*transnational conflicts*)

In addition, political conflicts can be categorized as power-political, socioeconomic or cultural conflicts according to the issues at hand:
- *Power-political conflicts* derive from the distribution of power, meaning access to positions of authority in state or society or within the international system.
- *Socioeconomic conflicts* revolve around the distribution of goods and rights within a nation-state or between nation-states as well as

around the distribution of related mechanisms. This group covers a range of conflicts, including those relating to resources.
- *Cultural conflicts* are conflicts in which culture is the issue. Not motives but themes are the decisive criteria here. In other words, a cultural conflict occurs when actors focus on cultural content in a conflictual manner. In this case, culture is seen as a "network of meaning" that is created to give rise to and preserve a collective identity.[1] Everything that is constructed by a society to produce and preserve its collective identity and that is subsequently construed as context by actors involved in a "communication situation"[2] belongs to the realm of the cultural.

By limiting the discussion to the realm of identity, we are using a definition of culture that is moderate in scope and that differentiates itself both from a narrow sociological notion (culture as a complex of standards, values and norms and their symbolization) and from the extended ethnological concept (culture as the definition of the human way of life per se). The advantage of this identity-focused definition lies in its practical nature. It references exactly that subsection of reality that is of interest when analyzing political conflicts, that is, identity.

Cultural dimensions and conflict fields

The genesis and preservation of a collective identity is linked to three prerequisites (Smelser 1992: 11; Hansen 2000: 47; Luhmann 1984: 224, 1985: 46 f.):
- The world's and society's complexity must be reduced to make identity possible (*symbolic complexity reduction*).

1 This operationalization of culture lies thus transversely to the cultural layers depicted by Fons Trompenaars and Charles Hampden-Turner (2002), who draw distinctions between explicit, normative and implicit cultures.
2 "Identity" is the result of a self-referential assignment of meaning, that is, the "self-conception" that arises from the interplay of the coherence of defining characteristics ("identity in a strict sense") and difference as differentiation from the other ("alterity") (cf. Gleason 1983).

- To be disseminated, identity must be communicated within the collective (*symbolic communication*).
- To be preserved, identity must be continously reproduced (*symbolic reproduction*).

In the human collective, these preconditions are inevitably achieved through the use of symbols (Dörner 2003: 603; Fleischer 2001: 307). Culture's three dimensions can be depicted together with their respective concrete domains in the following way:

Table 1: Culture's dimensions and domains

Dimension	Domain	Meaning
Symbolic complexity reduction	Religion	Contingency reduction, also in a postmortal/ transcendental perspective
	Ideology	Closed, this-worldly Weltanschauung
Symbolic communication	Language	Communication system as an automated component of culture
	Ritual	Identity-related, non-verbal act of communication
Symbolic reproduction	Historicity	Historicity/historical experience in the sense of distinctive historical events or factual/ historicized history of origin

Note: As it is used here, the concept of historicity is different from that used among historians, who understand it as the factual nature of historical events.

Confrontative communication in conventional political conflicts—that is, in those that do not focus on culture—refers to a given issue as the object of conflict. As a rule, an explicit demand is formulated as a discrete, limited, interest-driven conflict item, such as the demand to transfer a clearly delineated territorial area to the opposing side. In contrast, cultural conflicts do not focus on interests but on identity.

Cultural conflicts are identity conflicts. Thus, the conflict issue does not follow from what the actors want or purport to want but, rather, from what they are or believe themselves to be. Even if traditional conflict items almost always play an ancillary role, in a cultural conflict the communication situation centers on issues relating to identity that are not explicitly formulated (hereafter referred to as the "conflict field.")

The concept of the conflict field is an attempt to simultaneously accommodate "softer" and deeper objects of conflict in addition to "hard" demands, which are usually clearly formulated within the public discourse. It must be noted that both conflict items and conflict fields represent themes and not motives; they express what the conflict is about and what is being communicated rather than why the conflict is taking place, in the sense of what its underlying causes are (Seul 1999: 564). Examining thematic conflict issues also leaves open the question of whether actors are truly addressing the issues or whether they are instrumentalizing them for purposes that are not (publically) explained.

For the current study, the cultural domains of religion, language and historicity, as described above, have been taken as conflict fields. Culture's other domains—ideology and ritual—could not be utilized for practical, research-related reasons.[3]

The following indicators were used to operationalize the three conflict fields:

3 No information exists—let alone (even tendentially) comprehensive, quantifiable information—on adherents of given ideologies or on participants in given rituals. In addition, no conflicts are known to exist that focus on given rituals or on ritual per se. Ideology, in turn, presents another unique problem: Numerous conflicts exist that center on, for example, communist or nationalist ideologies. In all such instances, the conflict always targets state power and the state's resulting ideological bent. As such, this represents an indivisible connection between power and ideology. The conflict field disappears completely behind the conflict item and, as a result, it is no longer accessible for independent analysis.

Table 2: Operationalization of conflict fields

Conflict field	Indicator	Example
Religion	Verbal or active reference to a religious symbol (person or object) that is understood as referencing a religious issue	Controversial visit to a temple by a head of government or an attempt to assassinate a religious leader
Language	Verbal or active reference to a linguistic symbol (person or object) that is understood as referencing language	Prohibiting use of a language at a university or recognizing a dialect as its own language
Historicity	Verbal or active reference to a symbol (person or object) in relation to distinctive historical events or to the factual/historicized history of origin such that this reference is understood as referencing historicity	Controversial erection of a war memorial or public discourse on a state's pre-colonial past

Note: Skin color and physiognomy as issues (i.e., what has been described as "racial membership") also have their place within the historicitary conflict field. Given the slow disappearance of its distinctiveness, skin color is particularly "suited" to serve as a symbolic reminder of the history of origin.

This conception of cultural conflict is clearly different from other definitions commonly used in the field for denoting "ethnic" or "religious" conflicts.

"Ethnic conflicts" are political conflicts between ethnic groups or conflicts that involve at least one such group. The actors are an ethnic conflict's defining characteristic. Who they are, however, does not necessarily determine what they are communicating about; the conflict's content, its subject matter, is largely left in the dark. While an ethnic group is commonly defined in cultural terms (Eller 1999: 13), the assumption that ethnic groups are always and primarily fighting for their identity is a hasty conclusion. "Ethnic" conflicts can also center on conflict items relating to power politics or socioeconomic conditions. Such a situation is illustrated by the protests carried out by the Ogoni people in southeast Nigeria against Royal Dutch Shell and the Nigerian government. Although the conflict clearly divides along ethnic lines, the conflict issues are living conditions and the distribution of income from oil sales. Thus, not every ethnic conflict is a cultural conflict.

While it is imaginable that an ethnic group might function as an actor in the case of ethnic strife, the same is not plausible in the case of religious strife. Often an organized (usually non-state) party to the conflict serves as a replacement actor, one that is connected to the religion in question. It remains doubtful, however, whether the fact that a given organization consists exclusively of Hindus, Sikhs, Christians or Muslims suffices in and of itself for any conflict advanced by the group to be labeled "religious."

Cultural context as reference point for conflict communication: types of cultural conflict

The concept of "conflict measure" is understood to include every conflict-relevant act and statement made by an actor. The measure itself can be a one-time event, or it can extend over a longer period of time (for data generation within the CONIS project, cf. Croissant et al. 2009). Within the methodology of this study, conflict measures were used to estimate the significance of the conflict fields. What the actors do or say within the conflict itself was used to determine—based on an analytic interpretation of the relevant events—which topic was at the heart of the conflict.

In the case of identity-related conflict fields, the assessment of conflict measures is not only dependent on how such measures were intended, but also on how they were understood by the recipient. The destruction of Christian churches in Germany during World War II, for example, was (in accordance with the Allies' intentions) not perceived by either the populace or government leaders as making reference to a religious symbol and, accordingly, the war was not seen as a religious conflict. In addition to the actors' actions themselves, the actors' interpretations of their actions were also considered in the project.

The categorization of conflicts was dichotomous, that is, the question at hand was whether a cultural field was affected or not.[4] This resulted in the following possible conflict types:

---

4   If historicity becomes an issue in a conflict along with language or religion, then it is implicitly a topic, as part of the concrete language or religion. If, however, neither language nor religion is an issue and the conflict at hand nevertheless is a cultural one by virtue of its focus on identity, then historicity has been coded as the relevant conflict field.

Table 3: Possible conflict types

Conflict Type	Religion	Language	Historicity	Examples
Non-cultural conflict	0	0	0	East Timor vs. Australia and similar resource conflicts
Religious conflict	1	0	0	Israel (Israelis vs. Palestinians)
Linguistic conflict	0	1	0	Belgium (Flemings vs. Walloons)
Historicitary conflict	0	0	1	United Kingdom (Scotland vs. England)
Religious-linguistic conflict	1	1	0	Sri Lanka (Tamils vs. Singhalese)

Note: All other combinations of religion, language and historicity (0/1/1, 1/0/1 and 1/1/1) are covered by the coding rules (cf. footnote 4), that is, the more relevant component of religion or language vis-à-vis historicity is used for categorization.

In summary, a cultural conflict—in the sense of being a dependent variable—is classified along the three dimensions of religion, language and historicity. Hybrid forms are possible, although they are assigned to either the main dimensions of religion or language or to the mixed religious-linguistic conflict group.

Accordingly, determining whether a conflict should be seen as cultural and which thematic conflict type it should be assigned to depends on which issues at least one of the actors (e.g., a government) or an actor associated with it (e.g., a military commander) make reference to. Whether and in which form such references exist is determined by the actor's communicated intentions and by the communicated understanding of the message's recipient or recipients, that is, by the communications as documented in publically accessible sources.

A multistep procedure was used to identify and categorize each concrete conflict. Existing conflict measures were initially examined for each individual conflict to determine whether a cultural reference could be ascertained. A panel consisting of at least three evaluators analyzed each conflict before discussing the proposed classification. When a consensus was reached based on the materials at hand, the case was entered into one of the database tables in the form of a numeric code. All other conflicts were added as part of a secondary process, during which additional information was gathered on the conflict before the panel examined it once again. If no consensus was reached, an external expert was consulted.

This procedure of positive inclusion and the methodological limitation that no distinction can be made between strong and weak referencing bring with them the danger that cultural and non-cultural conflicts might not be differentiated robustly enough. As a result, two additional factors were used to classify the conflicts. First, the identification of the cultural nature of a conflict rests on the actions and utterances of the leading ranks of the parties to the respective conflict.

Second, the communications between the parties to the conflict were used to conclusively determine that the cultural conflict has been understood as such. A conscious decision was thus made not to use a simple numeric rule, with which a conflict would be classified as cultural or non-cultural based solely on the frequency with which the actors made reference to a conflict field. This was considered important since, ultimately, neither a general rule can be made (i.e., extrapolation from an individual case) as to how many references are required to assign a conflict to a specific category, nor can the number of references per se provide information on the significance of the conflict field since, for actors, "talk is cheap" (i.e., when communicating with third parties they can offer non-authentic reasons for their actions). Consequently, no theoretically justified threshold values can be provided within the process of empiric measurement to mark the boundary between distinct conflict types. Instead, the chosen process can be seen as a contextualizing and analytical interpretation of existing data.

This is made clear by the second war between the United States and Iraq. Although it has continued to be portrayed as such in the media, the war is not a cultural conflict. While certain statements (e.g., the use of the term "crusade" by leaders in the US) or actions (e.g., the humiliation of Iraqi prisoners at Guantánamo) do, in fact, suggest a cultural reference point for the conflict, it cannot be classified as a cultural conflict given the avoidance of the term on the part of the US president following criticism of its use, statements made by his advisors that they see no historical parallels to disputes between Christians and Muslims, and statements by US military leaders that they intended to investigate incidents at Guantánamo using legal channels and to punish any criminal behavior through the courts.

Cultural context as a reference point for conflict motivation: culture as a potential cause of conflict

As noted above, cultural context is a reference point for conflict communication. Based on culture's diverse domains, the conflict fields of religion, language and historicity provide cultural subject matter for political conflicts. In addition, the cultural context can be considered a reference point for the factors motivating the conflict and can thus be seen as a cause of conflict. In order to investigate this viewpoint, which is regularly encountered in research of culture and conflict, indicators of "ethnic fragmentation" (also known as ethnic diversity or heterogeneity) are often employed (Fearon and Laitin 2003; Collier and Hoeffler 2004).

Given the noted problems relating to the notion of ethnicity, such a method seems insufficient. To investigate whether cultural diversity in the form of linguistic or religious heterogeneity influences the genesis and intensity of conflict, this study employs a different approach for quantitatively assessing the cultural context: It identifies cultural fragmentation directly via quantitative data on religious or linguistic heterogeneity instead of examining a society's ethnic fragmentation using information on its ethnic groups per se.

Accordingly, the index of cultural fragmentation developed here is more of a composite index: Arithmetic means are calculated based on the linguistic and religious heterogeneity present in a given society.

To determine linguistic fragmentation, we used SIL International's "Ethnologue" dataset (Gordon 2005). This dataset presents each country's linguistic heterogeneity in the form of a diversity index developed by Joseph Greenberg, which shows the probability that two randomly chosen inhabitants of a given country will have different native languages.[5] The same equation is used for calculating religious fragmentation based on percentages supplied by the 2007 edition of the Encyclopaedia Britannica, which facilitates a comparison of data.

---

5   Index values lie between 0 and 1. A value of 0 signifies that all inhabitants in a country have the same native language, while a value of 1 signifies that every person has a different native language (Gordon 2005). The Greenberg Index is mathematically identical to the fragmentation index developed by Douglas Raes and Michael Taylor: $1-\Sigma(p_i)^2$ (Rae and Taylor 1970: 22 f.), where p_i represents the share of language i among the overall population (Dumont and Caulier 2003: 4).

Cultural Conflicts as a Subset of Global Conflicts Since 1945

As a second goal, this study aims to provide a complete representation of the globe's cultural conflicts in the period from 1945 to 2007. The classification of conflicts in one or more cultural conflict fields has been carried out based on the CONIS database.

The database

In creating the CONIS databank, information from publically accessible news sources has been qualitatively evaluated, making it suitable for event data analysis. In addition to examining actor-related structures—that is, which actors are present as well as their military, economic, institutional and sociocultural characteristics—the data shed light, first and foremost, on conflict measures. Compared to other empirical approaches to conflict research—such as the Correlates of War project (COW, cf. Singer and Small 1972; Small and Singer 1982; Sarkees 2000) and the Uppsala Conflict Data Program (UCDP, cf. Wallensteen and Sollenberg 2001; Harbom and Wallensteen 2007)—the data contained in the new CONIS conflict database offers information that is both more extensive and detailed since it covers all forms of political conflict around the globe since 1945 and is not limited to individual regions or violent conflicts.

In other aspects as well, CONIS offers more differentiated information than other comparable sources. It provides data on conflict dynamics, that is, the individual development phases of specific conflicts. In addition, it is a quantitative dataset (i.e., deriving from a large number of observed cases) of qualitative nature since, in contrast to other sources, it does not measure and classify conflicts based on the number of mortally wounded but, rather, on a substantive analysis of the communications and activities taking place among actors.

The dynamic conflict model developed for CONIS comprises five levels: The first (*"dispute"*) denotes the articulation of opposing interests, while the second (*"non-violent crisis"*) represents the threat of violence. The third level (*"violent crisis"*) denotes a sporadic, limited use of violence. In the fourth level (*"limited war"*), violence is used in a planned manner without having the goal of completely vanquishing the opposing side but, rather, of causing it to capitulate. The fifth level (*"war"*) is the systematic use of violence with the goal of defeating the opposing side and forcing it to submit to the victor's will (Schwank, forthcoming).

In a first attempt to represent global conflicts since 1945, Figure 1 depicts the global progression of violent conflicts, both domestic and interstate. This illustration is based on conflict levels 4 and 5 ("limited war" and "war"), which have been merged into the category "high-intensity conflicts," while level-3 conflicts ("violent crisis") are represented as "medium-intensity conflicts."

The graphic analysis makes clear that domestic high-intensity conflicts ("civil wars") have been much more prevalent than interstate conflicts since the start of the period under analysis. Until the mid-1990s, they can even be generally seen, with minor exceptions, as the most common form of conflict. Following that, with the reduction in domestic high-intensity conflicts, domestic conflicts of medium intensity—violent crises—begin playing a much more significant role, having become the globe's predominant form of conflict since 2002.

The number of interstate high-intensity conflicts reached its high point—six—at the end of the 1970s. The widespread disappearance

Figure 1: Conflict development, 1945–2007

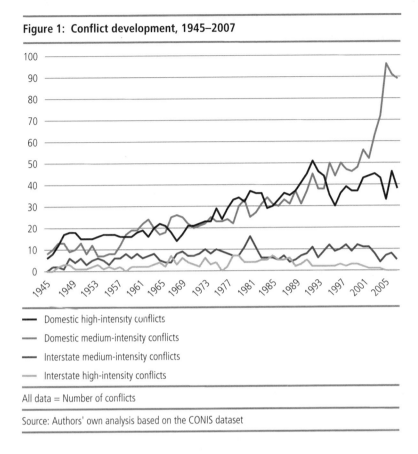

- — Domestic high-intensity conflicts
- — Domestic medium-intensity conflicts
- — Interstate medium-intensity conflicts
- — Interstate high-intensity conflicts

All data = Number of conflicts

Source: Authors' own analysis based on the CONIS dataset

of interstate wars, however, does not mean that tensions no longer exist among nation-states, which can be seen in the somewhat higher curve for interstate violent crises. The world's nations have apparently been successful at resolving tensions peacefully and, thereby, avoiding war.

First finding: cultural conflicts make up a high and increasing share of all conflicts

Using data from the CONIS database, a first attempt was made at examining the empiric foundations as well as the global and regional distribution of cultural conflicts. This examination showed that, of the 762 political conflicts found in CONIS in the period between 1945 and 2005, a total of 334, or almost 44 percent, can be classified as "cultural." When looking exclusively at the violent conflicts (i.e., levels 3 to 5), this share climbs to 50 percent (268 out of 534 conflicts). Figure 2 shows that the number of cultural conflicts first surpasses

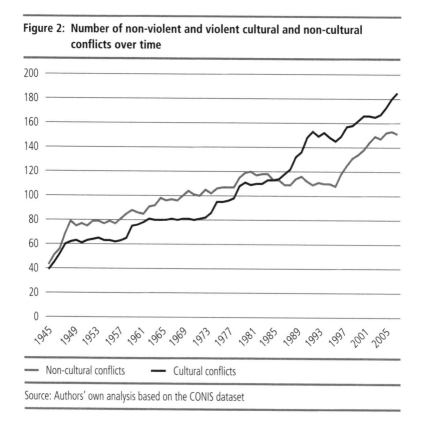

Figure 2: Number of non-violent and violent cultural and non-cultural conflicts over time

— Non-cultural conflicts   — Cultural conflicts

Source: Authors' own analysis based on the CONIS dataset

the number of non-identity-related conflicts in the mid-1980s (more exactly, as of 1986) and reaches its historical zenith in 2007.

This change in the global panorama of conflicts is based on two developments: the continuous, almost linear rise in cultural conflicts and, even more significantly, the relative stagnation in the number of non-cultural conflicts between 1979 and 1997. Only in the second half of the last decade do non-cultural conflicts once again increase in frequency, exhibiting a clear jump, even if they do not reach the level of cultural conflicts. The shift in the global conflict pattern is one possible cause for the increased interest that has been evident since the beginning of the 1990s among both specialists and the general public in domestic and, above all, ethnic conflicts as well as in cultural identity.

Second finding: cultural conflicts are primarily domestic

Cultural conflicts are clearly a domestic phenomenon. At 81 percent, the vast majority of cultural conflicts are to be found in the intrastate realm. In the case of conflicts carried out by violent means, this figure even rises to 86 percent. Although, cultural issues are evidently avoided on the international level, they dominate on the domestic level in terms of conflict communication. As Figure 3 makes clear, cultural conflicts make up less than 25 percent of interstate conflicts, while more than half of domestic conflicts have a cultural reference point.

Third finding:
the most common cultural conflicts are religious and historicitary

The 334 cultural conflicts divide into four categories: 165 (some 22 percent of all conflicts and over 49 percent of cultural conflicts) are historicitary; 86 (11 percent of all and almost 26 of cultural conflicts) are religious; 44 (6 percent of all and some 13 percent of cultural conflicts) are religious-linguistic; and 39 (5 percent of all and some 12 per-

Figure 3: Cultural conflicts as percentage of total domestic and interstate conflicts

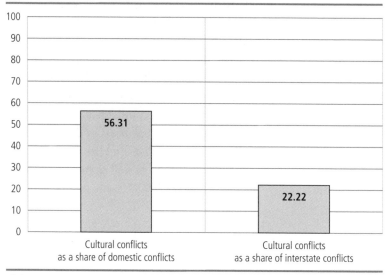

All data in percent

Source: Authors' own analysis based on the CONIS dataset

cent of cultural conflicts) are linguistic in nature. In other words, within the group of cultural conflicts, historicitary and religious conflicts dominate—despite the fact that, in line with the definition, their code only appears infrequently—while linguistic and "hybrid" conflicts are relatively rare.

Figure 4 shows two basic patterns that hold for both domestic and interstate conflicts. On the one hand, linguistic and religious-linguistic conflicts progress in a virtually identical manner. On the other, religious conflicts exhibit a highly unique pattern, beginning at the same point with linguistic and religious-linguistic conflicts in 1945 before diverging from them in 1965 in order to approach the level of historicitary conflicts by 2007.

Dividing individual cultural conflicts into domestic and interstate categories (as is done in Figure 5), it becomes apparent that historici-

Figure 4: Number of non-violent and violent political conflicts by type of conflict over time

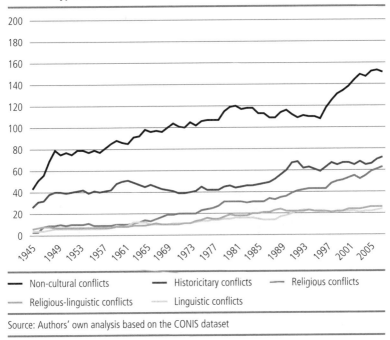

—— Non-cultural conflicts	—— Historicitary conflicts	—— Religious conflicts
—— Religious-linguistic conflicts	—— Linguistic conflicts	

Source: Authors' own analysis based on the CONIS dataset

tary conflicts—at 26 percent domestic and 13 percent interstate—are the most common type, followed by religious and religious-linguistic conflicts. Linguistic conflicts follow in last place, and it is notable that they are virtually non-existent among interstate conflicts.

Fourth finding: cultural conflicts are particularly violent

Examined according to their level of intensity—that is, their level of violence—it becomes clear that cultural and non-cultural conflicts exhibit contrasting characteristics (Figure 6). While non-cultural conflicts predominate at the lower levels, cultural conflicts are most present

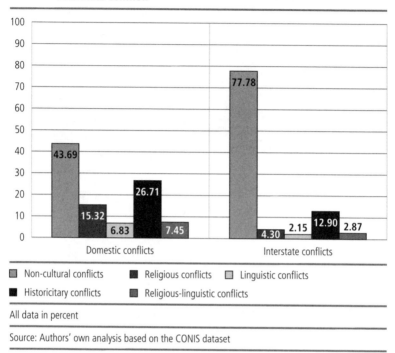

Figure 5: Individual conflict types as a percentage of total domestic and interstate conflicts

All data in percent

Source: Authors' own analysis based on the CONIS dataset

in the categories of "limited war" and "war." It can also be seen that the share of non-cultural conflicts declines progressively as the level of intensity increases, while the share of cultural conflicts rises progressively. This is particularly true of interstate conflicts.

Fifth finding: there are major differences between regions

In the domestic category, the distribution of individual conflict types across different global regions shows that non-cultural conflicts predominate in North and South America, while religious conflicts are highly prevalent in the Middle East. In Europe, on the other hand, linguistic conflicts are relatively common. Historicitary conflicts, in turn,

Figure 6: Share of non-violent and violent cultural and non-cultural conflicts by degree of intensity

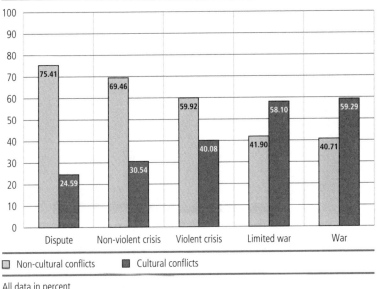

All data in percent

Source: Authors' own analysis based on the CONIS dataset

are especially typical for Asia and Africa. Finally, the American hemisphere completely lacks religious-linguistic strife (see Figure 7).

In the interstate category, as well, the Americas are primarily home to non-cultural conflicts. Again, religious conflicts are typical of the Middle East, while linguistic conflicts predominate in Europe, and historicitary conflicts are common in both Europe and the Middle East. Religious-linguistic conflicts, moreover, do not exhibit a dominant regional pattern. With regard to conflicts between states, it must be noted that the number of interstate conflicts, especially interstate cultural conflicts, is so small that no graphic representation has been undertaken here.

Figure 7: Domestic conflicts as share of conflict type by region

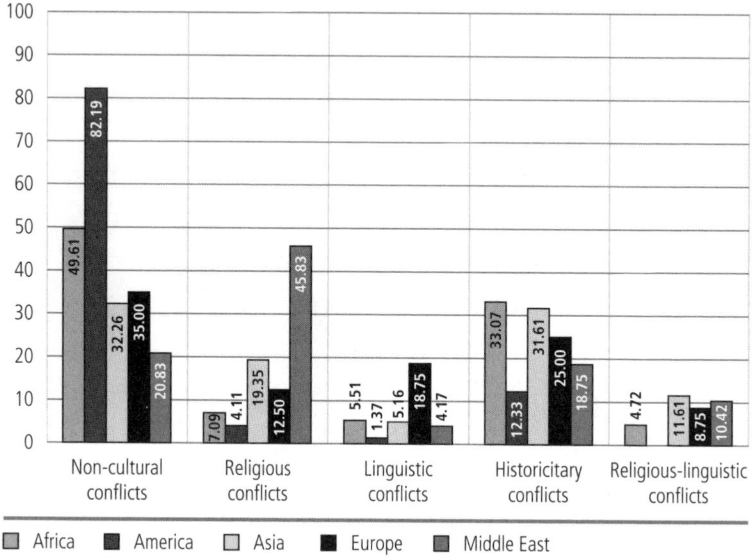

100
90
80
70
60
50
40
30
20
10
0

Non-cultural conflicts — 49.61, 82.19, 32.26, 35.00, 20.83
Religious conflicts — 7.09, 4.11, 19.35, 12.50
Linguistic conflicts — 5.51, 1.37, 5.16, 18.75, 4.17
Historicitary conflicts — 33.07, 31.61, 25.00, 18.75, 12.33, 45.83
Religious-linguistic conflicts — 4.72, 11.61, 8.75, 10.42

□ Africa   ■ America   □ Asia   ■ Europe   ▨ Middle East

All data in percent

Source: Authors' own analysis based on the CONIS dataset

Topography of cultural conflicts within the observation period

The findings found in this study are global in nature. They illustrate the developments, structures and occurrences of varying forms of cultural conflict around the world and over an extended period of time. Regional trends complement the global picture. At the same time, the findings do not provide conclusive information about cultural conflicts on the level of individual countries or societies. In light of that, we close this summary of empirical findings with a brief look at the nation-state level.

The following section presents two global maps depicting cultural conflicts. The assignment of index values makes clear the extent to which individual nations are encumbered by domestic cultural conflicts of medium intensity (conflict level 3, see Figure 8) and high intensity (conflict levels 4 and 5, see Figure 9). The index values range from 0 to 1, where a value of 1 signifies that a country has, in any given year, experienced at least one domestic cultural conflict of medium intensity. A value of 0 signifies that the country has never experienced such a conflict in any year. The color used to identify each country reflects the index value assigned to that country; white represents a value of 0, and dark gray represents a value of 1.

Based on the index calculations, countries that have been heavily affected include Angola, Eritrea, India, Iran, Namibia and Nigeria. Countries in Europe with relatively high values include Spain, given the conflict relating to the Basque region, and France, as a result of violence carried out by Corsican separatists. European nations, however, are only subject to one conflict and not multiple, parallel situations, as is the case in Africa or Asia.

In terms of highly violent conflicts around the globe, Figure 9 shows that the countries of Eritrea, Indonesia and Sudan have particularly high index values. The United Kingdom has, for European standards, an especially high value, a fact explained by the decades-long strife involving the Irish Republican Army (IRA) in Northern Ireland. As the country indices and maps show, the globe's conflicts are distributed very unevenly across individual countries, with some having none or very few cultural conflicts and others having been affected by such conflicts throughout their entire existence.

To be sure, these findings remain largely abstract. Historical case studies would be needed to provide insight into individual instances going beyond showing the characteristics of the phenomena found here. Within the scope of this study, which focuses on global developments, such analysis was possible only to a very limited extent.

42

Figure 8: Medium-intensity domestic cultural conflicts worldwide

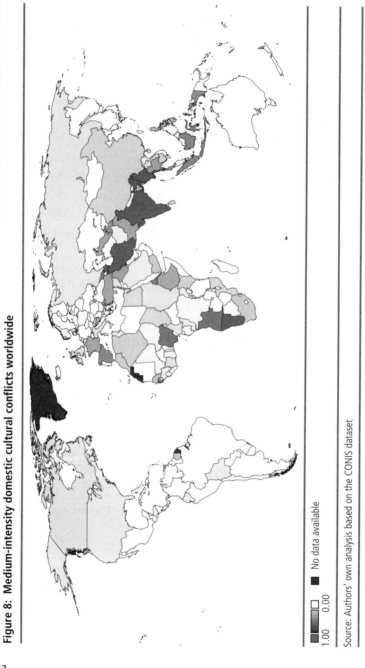

1.00
0.00
No data available

Source: Authors' own analysis based on the CONIS dataset

Figure 9: High-intensity domestic cultural conflicts worldwide

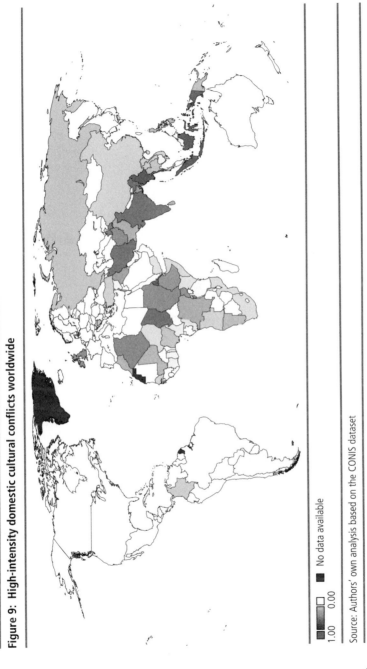

1.00   0.00   ■ No data available

Source: Authors' own analysis based on the CONIS dataset

43

Case Studies

We now present four brief case studies. They represent a more comprehensive sample of qualitative cases carried out as part of the overall study (Croissant et al. 2009) and having three closely interconnected objectives. First, these individual instances are meant to make clear how the concept of cultural conflicts—which focuses on conflict issues as opposed to causes—was approached in the empirical portion of this study. Second, they elucidate the significance of cultural factors (e.g., religion, language, historicity) relative to other relevant explanatory factors used in theoretically and empirically based conflict research. Third and finally, the cases discussed here are meant to illustrate the process—referred to here as "introference"—whereby cultural characteristics (e.g., religion, language and historicity) make themselves felt within a conflict.

Given the structure in which the chosen case studies are presented, the empirical scope of the following discussion is, of course, limited. At the same time, the case studies illustrate well the heuristic efficacy of our conceptual and theoretical assumptions. Four conflicts have thus been chosen: ones in Indonesia (Aceh), Belgium and Nigeria as well as that regarding the Danish cartoons depicting the Prophet Mohammed. The first three are domestic confrontations involving historicitary, linguistic or religious issues; the fourth is exemplary of transnational, religious conflicts.

These brief exposés are meant, above all, to show how cultural factors can become issues in specific empirical conflicts and transform situations into "cultural conflicts." They thereby also introduce a change in perspective as it pertains to the causes of cultural conflict. As was discussed earlies, this is one of this study's objectives, and it will serve as the focus of this paper's third section.

As is extensively documented by findings from descriptive studies of domestic and interstate conflicts carried out over the past six decades or so, culture plays an important role in the globe's many conflicts. Yet other factors are also germane and do much to explain strife as it manifests itself around the globe. A considerable fraction of the world's conflicts are non-cultural in nature, above all at the interstate level, and other structural factors have considerable explanatory relevance. The following case studies confirm these conclusions. None of the four conflicts, however, can be explained by cultural variables alone.

The Aceh conflict as an example of historicitary cultural conflict

Aceh, the most northernmost province on the island of Sumatra, is the setting for one of the oldest domestic conflicts in Indonesia as well as

Sumatra

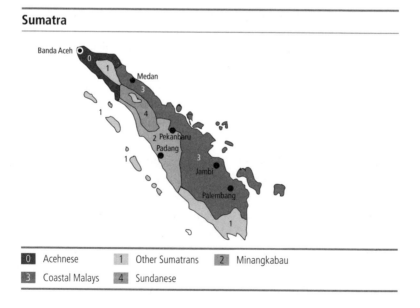

	0	Acehnese		1	Other Sumatrans		2	Minangkabau
	3	Coastal Malays		4	Sundanese			

all of Southeast Asia. The armed conflict in its narrower sense—that is, the dispute between the Gerakan Aceh Merdeka (Free Aceh Movement, or GAM) and the Indonesian state—began in 1976 with GAM's founding and its call for a Republic of Aceh independent of Indonesia.

Among conflict researchers, Aceh is depicted as a resource war as well as an "ethno-nationalist" and "ethno-religious" conflict (Searle 2002; Bertrand 2004a; Ross 2005). These divergent assessments point to the conflict's multifaceted nature and the complex, interrelated causalities underlying the situation.

Cultural factors make up the core of the independence movement's national self-definition: the common language, the strict interpretation of Islamic practices in Aceh, the memory of the pre-colonial sultanate of Aceh and the province's role in the struggle against Dutch colonial powers and for an Islamic Republic of Indonesia in the early phase of Indonesian independence. Economic factors also play a key role in how the conflict is perceived, as GAM's inception coincides with the start of the exploitation of the province's considerable oil and gas reserves. Indeed, quite a broad consensus exists among researchers that the conflict is based on inequalities and other causes that are material in nature and that derive from the conflict's structural context (Missbach 2005; Schulze 2006; Hadiwinata 2006).

A close observation of the conflict's dynamics and development, however, shows that, since violence broke out well over three decades ago, the dispute has taken on the clear characteristics of a cultural conflict. The roots of this development can be found in the transformation of the economic and political disagreements into cultural issues on the part of GAM and a significant portion of the local population. As part of this process, very real problems became the basis for a culturally referenced construction of Acehnese identity (*keacehan*, cf. Aspinall 2007; McCarthy 2007). In other words, cultural factors are not primarily relevant as the conflict's causes but, rather, as reference points for the creation of a separate identity, which has taken place over the course of GAM's political mobilization of the local population and the legitimizing of its goals and conflict strategies.

The strong identification with the Republic of Indonesia previously present in Acehnese society was weakened by economic inequality and discrimination, the lack of opportunities for political participation and repression (which, in turn, contained an ethnic component). This laid the foundation for the rise of GAM from its initial appearance as a marginal movement to its emergence as the representative of the province's desire for national self-determination and for maintaining its cultural identity. In addition, by making use of the population's dissatisfactions and using them as the point of departure for its construction of a cultural ("ethno-national") identity for Aceh, GAM played a key role in lending existing social problems cultural significance. The conflict surrounding the distribution of economic and political rights in the region was thus integrated into the broader process of constructing an identity (Aspinall 2007; Brown 2005; McCarthy 2007). GAM's political articulation of this identity has been successful, above all, by making reference to cultural definitions and symbols.

Found in the relevant literature among other locations, the viewpoint maintaining that GAM is merely instrumentalizing existing problems by misusing cultural issues to mobilize locals—as a way of achieving the group's "real" objectives of gaining power and influence (McCulloch 2005; Missbach 2005)—insufficiently depicts the role that culture plays in the conflict. While GAM is, indeed, not a genuine Islamist group in that it is not dedicated to introducing an Islamic social order or Islamic rule (Hadiwinata 2006: 7; Schulze 2004: 9), it has only been able to mobilize support for its goal of national independence because the vast majority of Aceh's population also views the existing problems as symptomatic of the lack of respect accorded to its identity (Bertrand 2004b: 173).

The Indonesian government's unwillingness to recognize this identity serves as the primary justification for the movement's call for secession. The fact that the conflict in Aceh also centers on concrete conflict items such as access to political power and the distribution of economic resources and other life opportunities is completely compatible with the interpretation of the conflict as a cultural or "culturalized" one. The question of recognizing or not recognizing an Acehnese identity was not present from the start but, instead, became a focal point over the course of the conflict's development.

> This constructivist viewpoint suggests that although it cannot originally be traced back to cultural factors, the conflict in Aceh is in fact a "cultural" or, more precisely, a "historicitary" conflict.

Similar to other manifestations of political disagreement, cultural conflicts are anchored in a social context. Although the struggle for concrete items (e.g., control over specific territory, access to resources or the distribution of political power) can play a significant role, the communication between actors in a cultural conflict focuses on religion, language or history—that is, the topics critical to identity.

Still GAM's "invention of tradition" (Sherlock 2005) is by no means limited to religious elements. Instead, the group propagated an Acehnese identity that was heavily historical in orientation, one that references linguistic unity, ancestral heritage, the common history of the pre-colonial sultanate and resistance to the Dutch (Schulze 2004: 7; 2006: 242) in addition to the strict observation of Islamic practices (in contrast to the more syncretistic Islam practiced on Java, in particular).

In this way, the movement has apparently succeeded in creating a plausible connection in the minds of many between the political and economic marginalization of the Acehnese population, on the one hand, and its cultural traditions and national identity, on the other. That the identity of this tradition and its components have to some extent been "invented" and, thereby, turned GAM into a representative of an identity that it itself has created (Sherlock 2005: 176, 187) is, of course, correct, even if it does nothing to alter the finding that culture has become an issue in the conflict after 32 years of armed strife.

Belgium's linguistic conflict

Belgium

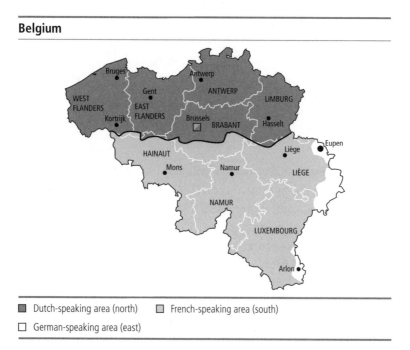

■ Dutch-speaking area (north)   □ French-speaking area (south)
□ German-speaking area (east)

The recent crisis following the parliamentary elections on June 10, 2007 clearly revealed Belgium's deep divisions. The country was deemed "ungovernable" (Proissl 2007), "no common denominator" was purported to exist anymore (de Coorebyter 2007) and the kingdom was said to stand "on the verge of division" (Müller-Thederan 2007). Yves Leterme's attempt to form a government took a difficult nine months, and his efforts were unable to prevent a new crisis shortly after he took office. Early in the summer of 2008, after only four months, Leterme's government fell since its main goal, a state reform designed to regulate relations between Flemings and Walloons, remained unachieved.

In addition, Belgium's linguistic conflict makes clear that cultural conflicts also take place in constitutional democracies, even if they tend to be resolved there in a more peaceful manner. In the CONIS database, Belgium reached its highest value—level 2, or non-violent crisis—in 2007. At the same time, the dispute in Belgium is one of the most acute cultural conflicts currently taking place. Even though it has strong historical roots that have been reinforced by socioeconomic inequalitie, it is primarily driven by language differences.

For centuries, the Flemings were the subgroup that was disadvantaged politically and economically, a state of affairs that reversed itself by the 1960s at the latest. In 2005, the Flemings earned some €8,000 more per capita in GDP than the Walloons. Data stretching back to the 14th century testify more to the differences between the Dutch-speaking Flemings and the French-speaking Walloons than to commonalities. For example, the victory of Flemish craftsmen over an army of French knights on July 11, 1302 is still being celebrated as a national holiday in Flanders.

Given its linguistic and historicitary aspects, the dispute between the Flemings and the Walloons can be identified primarily all as a cultural conflict. At the same time, the cultural components alone are not sufficient to depict the conflict's complex tapestry of causes but, instead, must be augmented by institutional and economic factors.

Belgium's restructuring from a centralized to a federal state and the complex institutional relationships among individual entities can be understood less as an originating cause of conflict than as the institutional result of the strife between the Flemings and Walloons. The federalization of the Belgian state and the search (which continues today) for a suitable institutional form (Swenden, Brans and De Winter 2006: 865) is an attempt to channel the conflict politically. The federal state, constitutionally anchored since 1993, allows for regional solutions that take Belgium's linguistic and cultural diversity into account. At the same time, the institutional structure cements the country's division and, by offering only a weak pan-Belgian identity, harbors the danger of institutionalizing the conflict, promoting centrifugal forces and accelerating the country's dissolution.

The centrifugal force emanating from the vertical division of state power is reinforced by the fragmentation of the Belgian party system, which has not been home to national party organizations since the late 1970s and which is the most fragmented party system found among Western democracies. Separate francophone and Flemish party structures that mirror the country's regional and linguistic borders have been formed (cf. De Winter, Swyngedouw and Dumont 2006: 933).

This fragmentation is a threat to the kingdom's stability since it vastly amplifies problems of coordination and makes it considerably more difficult to create national coalitions, as recent history has shown. For example, the average number of parties included in a government rose from 1.8 before 1968 to a current 4.4. In addition, the time it took to negotiate the formation of a coalition government doubled between 1968 and 2003 to a current 43 days (cf. De Winter and Dumont 2006: 958). Destabilizing tendencies have become increasingly apparent even within the Green Party, which up until 2003 attempted to maintain a multilinguistic parliamentary group in the national parliament and to combat cross-regional problems with national programs. In addition, problems have also ensued as a result of multiple election campaigns' taking place within any given legislative period, as national and regional elections now follow separate timetables. This, too, has increased polarization.

Language plays a key role in the dispute between Flemings and Walloons. In Belgium today, some 60 percent of the population speaks Dutch, almost 40 percent speaks French and less than 1 percent speaks German. With the exception of Brussels, the country's capital, linguistic borders are identical with the country's regional and administrative borders, giving rise to the conflict's territorial manifestation.

For both subgroups, but especially for the Flemings, speaking one's own language is an expression of regional and cultural identity as well as of equality within the country's political system. In addition, language is the decisive factor when it comes to creating each "sphere of communication" (Rochtus 1998: 5) and forming identities of "us" and "them." The language difference is not the only factor in the dispute between Flemings and Walloons, but it brings together a number of the conflict's diverse causes and has proven to be the key focal point because it offers an unmistakable, high-profile criterion for distinguishing one subgroup from another (Hecking 2003: 70).

For Flemings, language has taken on a central role in the struggle for linguistic, political and socioeconomic equality. In the 19th century, for example, the "Flemish movement" derived a majority of its legitimacy from efforts to prevent discrimination against the Dutch language, which was long considered merely a collection of dialects spoken by peasants, and the related oppression of the Flemish population. The language issue and efforts to accord Dutch equal status then converged with a desire to do away with the primacy accorded to the French-speaking bourgeoisie and the socioeconomic oppression of the Flemings, with the result that the conflict's linguistic dimension occasionally took on the characteristics of a class struggle.

Two developments stand out in the period during which the Dutch language was accorded equality through its designation as a second official language and during which the Flemings gained in political strength through the introduction, at the end of the 19th century, of an electoral code based on majority rule. First, the linguistic conflict took on a clear territorial bent, separating Flanders from Wallonia. Second, not only did this development reinforce notions of a Flemish identity, it also fueled the Walloons' identification with their own linguistic community and provoked a counter-reaction in the form of a "Walloon movement." The more the Flemings repudiated all things French in Belgium's north—for example, by eliminating bilingualism in Flanders to the detriment of the French language—and the more the Walloons began to fear the specter of a Dutch-speaking Belgium, the more a Walloon identity began to take shape and, with it, opposing attitudes in the different linguistic groups (cf. Strikwerda 1997: 37).

As a result, two major cultural communities exist in Belgium today, and there are also two largely self-contained spheres of communication, which provide both linguistic groups with different cultural and political reference points while hindering any reinforcement of a pan-Belgian identity and, consequently, exacerbating the situation in "Babel on the North Sea" (Hecking 2003: 71).

The extent to which linguistic barriers are present in everyday life is demonstrated by two examples heatedly debated within the country. First, in 1982, the Flemish authorities refused to recognize a francophone candidate who had been elected mayor of the town of Fouron, justifying their actions by saying he did not speak Dutch (Falter 1998: 187). On-the-ground linguistic obstacles were discussed a second time in 2001, when two trains collided because the railway employees responsible for switching the tracks had reportedly not been able to communicate with each other (Hecking 2003: 71).

Still, beyond the factors promoting Belgium's fragmentation, other forces—in addition to the triad of king, art and soccer—can be seen as holding the country together (Berger 2005). The mechanisms for seeking consensus at the national level, for example, help prevent a complete fragmentation of the country. This is reinforced by the fact that a national office is still considered desirable by regional politicians. A further deterrent to disintegration is the fear of having to address yet again the question of what would happen to the city of Brussels should the country break apart. Finally, Belgium's position as a solid member of the European Union, which is supported by a majority of Belgians, also works against the country's dissolution (Chardon 2007). However, it remains to be seen whether these factors will be sufficient in the long run to dampen the conflict between the country's linguistic factions and turn Belgium into a stable federal state.

Ethno-regional and religious conflict in Nigeria

Nigeria

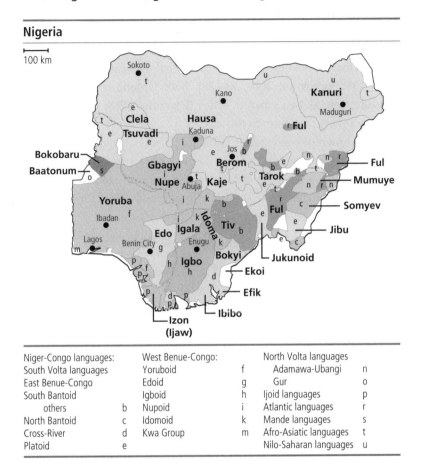

Niger-Congo languages:		West Benue-Congo:		North Volta languages	
South Volta languages		Yoruboid	f	Adamawa-Ubangi	n
East Benue-Congo		Edoid	g	Gur	o
South Bantoid		Igboid	h	Ijoid languages	p
others	b	Nupoid	i	Atlantic languages	r
North Bantoid	c	Idomoid	k	Mande languages	s
Cross-River	d	Kwa Group	m	Afro-Asiatic languages	t
Platoid	e			Nilo-Saharan languages	u

Culturally speaking, Nigeria is a highly fragmented country. Researchers have identified more than 250 ethnic groups (Chukwuma 1985: 39; Akinwumi 2004: 20). At the same time, the country's ethnic fragmentation is asymmetrical: Almost 30 percent of Nigeria's inhabitants belong to the Muslim Hausa-Fulani in the country's north, some 20 percent to the Yoruba—who are half Muslim and half Christian—in the southwest, and over 15 percent to the mostly Christian Igbo in the southeast (Diamond 1988: 22).

Nigerian history, in its modern phase, begins in the 19th century with the British colonial presence. The majority of today's Nigeria was divided into two regions (protectorates), which corresponded to the areas settled by the Hausa-Fulani, on the one hand, and the Igbo and Yoruba, on the other. Despite their legal unification (Chukwuma 1985: 195; Akinwumi 2004: 21, 28), both regions continued to be ruled de facto as two separate states (Diamond 1988: 26), a division that essentially continues to this day.

An ethno-regional conflict paradigm has characterized Nigeria's history since independence. The conflict lines run between subnational regions, which are defined along political and geographical lines and dominated by a specific ethnic group. The ethno-regional lines of conflict continue to reflect the country's colonial division into northern and southern regions.

The north-south division is not based on linguistic and also not primarily on religious differences[6] but, rather, on history. The British had a much larger political and cultural influence on the south than on the north, a development that also had a major socioeconomic impact. While the south was "better-educated" and, above all, economically better-off, the north was seen as more "conservative" and less-developed (Chukwuma 1985: 211; Diamond 1988: 27 f.; Harnisch-feger 2006: 56). This description remains valid today.

The north-south division is superimposed by opposing demographic and geographic factors. The country's northern region has had and continues to have a significantly larger population than the south, and, in terms of territory, is almost three times the size. This continues to tip the scales of power in favor of the north, even, and especially, under democratic conditions (Chukwuma 1985: 49; Diamond 1988: 292; Harnischfeger 2006: 66 ff., 123 ff.). The combination

---

6   For example, both Muslims and Christians can be found among the Yoruba, and the southern part of the country's northern region—known as the "Middle Belt"—is inhabited by numerous ethnic minorities, most of whom are Christian. In addition, adherents of "traditional" forms of belief continue to be found in all three major ethnic groups.

of the north's socioeconomic weakness and its political dominance has created the preconditions for using Nigeria's national structures and resources to this region's advantage (Diamond 1988: 293; Akinwumi 2004: 20).

This disparity resulted in the demise of the country's first republic, only three years after independence, in the form of a military coup carried out in 1966 by Igbo leaders. In the same year, however, a counter-putsch took place led by Hausa-Fulani, resulting in the deaths of tens of thousands of Igbo living in the north (Harnischfeger 2006: 68 f.). The Nigerian Civil War, which lasted from 1967 to 1970, broke out as a result. The conflict, also known as the Biafra War, was fought in an attempt to secure independence for the Republic of Biafra, with its Igbo majority, and was ultimately won by Nigeria.

In a certain sense, the Biafra War represents the zenith of Nigeria's ethno-regional disputes. While ethno-regional conflicts continued to play a role following the war, as they do today (Harnischfeger 2006: 118–123), the conflict-determining factors of "region and religion" have swung about since the end of the 1980s, with disputes between Muslims and Christians moving into the forefront.

A key reason for the shift from an ethno-regional to a religious conflict paradigm can be found in ethno-political learning processes. The Biafra War made clear to both parties to the conflict that an escalation of ethno-regional conflicts has highly undesirable consequences. We advance here the supposition that the transformation to a religious conflict paradigm was an immediate result of this ethno-political learning process, with the widespread discrediting of the ethno-regional conflict paradigm ultimately requiring Nigeria's power-political and socioeconomic tensions to break through in another guise.

This supposition seems particularly compelling since, during the commencement of the religious conflict paradigm in the first half of the 1980s, violent strife prevailed among various Muslim groups and claimed thousands of lives (Harnischfeger 2006: 72 ff.). The disputes included the uprisings in Kano in 1980 and 1982, as well as those in Maiduguri in 1982, in Jimeta in 1984 and in Gombe in 1985 (Akinwumi 2004: 147).

The first disturbances between Muslims and Christians followed directly in Ilorin and Ibadan in 1986, in Kaduna and Kafanchan in 1987, and in Bauchi, Kano and Katsina in 1991 (Akinwumi 2004: 147). It seems all too likely that the basic pattern, which became apparent in the intra-Muslim conflicts, namely the emphasis on decidedly religious issues, was adapted to the inter-ethnic, inter-regional conflict situation, thus transforming it into an inter-religious conflict constellation. Focusing on decidedly religious content was "learned" from the intra-Muslim system of conflicts and transferred to the inter-religious realm.

If the religious conflict paradigm has supplanted the ethno-regional one, it does not mean that the causes underlying the ethno-regional conflicts have disappeared or that religion has simply become the cause of conflict. The causes of both paradigms must, instead, be seen in the north-south development divide in conjunction with the south-north power divide. The causes of conflict thus clearly derive from sociopolitical conditions and power politics. At the same time, however, the way these causes are portrayed has shifted. In earlier decades, the disputes were seen primarily from a historicitary viewpoint, with the focus originally put on the different heritage of the Hausa, Fulani, Yoruba and Igbo and their different pre-colonial and colonial histories. Within the religious paradigm, the historical perspective is relinquished in favor of religious aspects.

In the religious paradigm, virulent causes of conflict are emphasized using clearly religious content. One catalyzing issue has thus become the conflict over the introduction of Shariah (i.e., Islamic law) and its applicability to various areas of life, as well as its territorial application. The basic reason for the recently made demand (Ahanotu 1992: 73; Okafor 1992: 159 ff.; Harnischfeger 2006: 72) to introduce—or re-introduce—Shariah and for its ultimate success can be found in the "ideologization of Islam" (Esposito 1988: 169) and its insistence on subjecting all areas of life to religious belief.

These reservations vis-à-vis secularism are also not foreign to Nigeria's Christians. Igbo and Yoruba, however, favor the model of a secular, religiously neutral state (Ahanotu 1992: 16 f.), less from an inner conviction than from the consideration that, given the north's preeminent position, having a centralized state that is secular can permanently prevent the north from instrumentalizing it to serve Muslim and northern interests.

In addition to the possible application of Shariah to non-Muslims, the Nigerian discourse on Islamic law impacts, above all, Nigeria's juristic and territorial cohesion. Three aspects are of key significance here: First, application of different legal codes accentuates the country's lack of inner coherence and, as a result, the basic failure of the efforts to create a Nigerian nation-state (Afigbo 2005; Harnischfeger 2006: 251 f.).

Second, equal protection under the law is no longer a reality in Nigeria, which has negative consequences for non-Muslims, who face discrimination, and for those Muslims, who must live according to Shariah's more stringent legal and social requirements (Harnischfeger 2006: 108).

Third, state institutions are applying non-state law (at the internal state level; Muslims have long demanded the introduction of a Shariah court at the national level in order to ensure standardized interpretation of Sharia law; Harnischfeger 2006: 75). This erodes the state's norm-setting monopoly since, from the perspective of Shariah, (legitimate) state structures do not derive from a social contract among humans but, rather, from divine will (Harnischfeger 2006: 157 f.).

For a county like Nigeria, whose existence has resulted from Western state power and from a Western concept of state and which is essentially bipolar in religious respects, this development can be seen as a major risk to its legitimacy. The resulting deficit in legitimacy of the nation-state, moreover, paves the way for political conflict. Treating causes of conflict arising from socioeconomic conditions and power politics as cultural issues ultimately leads to a reification of the discourse. In other words, treating non-cultural causes of conflict as cultural becomes itself a cause of additional conflict.

The 2005 conflict over Danish cartoons depicting Mohammed

On September 30, 2005, the Danish newspaper *Morgenavisen Jyllands-Posten* printed 12 cartoons, most of which included a depiction of Mohammed, the Islamic prophet. Together with an article that appeared in the same issue discussing the increasing caution that Western media were exercising in dealing with the subject of Islam, this represented the start of a political conflict that—given its rapid expansion across the globe, the willingness of some participants to engage in public violence and the clear lines separating Western and Muslim societies—seemed to serve as a prototype for Huntington's prophesied "clash of civilizations."

In light of its almost exclusive reference to religious symbols and the simultaneous appearance of both state and non-state actors, this conflict has a special significance for this study, a significance that is further augmented by the conflict's being carried out in multiple countries all at once and, as a result, its being the only transnational conflict among the cases portrayed here. Yet can it truly be seen as inherently part of a clash of civilizations? And are similar conflicts to be expected in the future?

Why did the escalation occur? After Muslims in Denmark complained in October 2005 to the country's prime minister, Anders Fogh Rasmussen, about publication of the cartoons to no avail (Schlötzer 2006), a delegation of Danish Muslims traveled in December of the same year to Lebanon and Qatar in order to call attention in the Arab Islamic world to what they perceived to be the Islamophobia prevailing in Denmark (ibid.). The tension that resulted in a number of Arab countries then increased after the cartoons were published once again in Norwegian newspapers at the beginning of January 2006, an event that produced a number of other reactions, including the Saudi Arabian ambassador's being recalled from Copenhagen.

Publication of the cartoons on February 2 and 3, 2006 in other newspapers in Europe and beyond ignited the situation once more. Following Friday prayers on February 3, protests erupted in Pakistan,

Indonesia, Iran and other Middle Eastern countries (Ramelsberger and Kessler 2006). The demonstrators burned Danish flags and chanted "death to Denmark" (ibid.). Demonstrations took place on the same day in Europe as well, most of which remained peaceful.

The feelings in Arab Muslim states, however, were purposefully stoked. Sheik Yusuf al-Qaradawi—the Egyptian chairman of the International Union of Muslim Scholars, a member of the Muslim Brotherhood, a popular television preacher and the operator of the website islamonline.net—had previously used the Internet and his television program on Al Jazeera to urge Muslims around the world to use February 3 as a "day of anger," a suggestion also endorsed by France's Muslim Council. Violent protests outside of Europe claimed more than 100 lives that day. The virulence of the protests even seemed to surprise the Muslim world's leaders and, around the globe, they endeavored to de-escalate the situation, despite the previous calls for all of the globe's Muslims to show their anger.

The frequency of the protests declined as of March 2006, even if isolated demonstrations continued to occur through May 2008, including a foiled attempt to assassinate an artist who drew one of the cartoons, Kurt Weestergard (Reimann 2008).

Especially from a Western perspective, it remains unclear to this day why this conflict gave rise to such turbulent reactions. To most people in Europe's secular countries, printing cartoons depicting the Prophet Mohammed seems too minor an event to cause so many protests of such intensity.

In point of fact, two key complementary factors caused the conflict to escalate. The first is the deliberate provocation by Danish and, later, other Western newspapers, designed to precipitate a discussion of the media's purported self-censorship when it comes to issues relating to Islam. The second is the agitation carried out by several Muslim religious and political leaders, who were more than willing to be provoked and who quickly helped disseminate the cartoons, since they saw them as confirmation of their own prejudices vis-à-vis Western culture and wanted to defend themselves against what they perceived to be an insult to their beliefs.

As can be seen, the cause of the escalation was not the cartoons' publication alone. The reason the protests took on the scale they did can be found in the cultural framework in which the conflict unfolded and which was supplied by the parties to the conflict. From the very beginning, Denmark's Muslims made clear that they felt their religious views had been impugned and that the clash over the cartoons was more than a purely political affair. They perceived the depiction of the Prophet Mohammed to be disrespectful and to denote a lack of recognition of their religious values.

For Denmark's Muslim immigrants, an additional political aspect also played a role, in that they expect the Danish state to defend religious values and prevent a repetition of the offending activities or similar events, as Muslim states would. Not only did this expectation remain unfulfilled, it met with complete bafflement, since the Danish public perceived the Muslim protests as a rejection of the country's established social rights and values, such as freedom of the press and separation of church and state. The religious meaning that the publication of the cartoons had for Muslims was lost on large parts of Danish society, including many of its politicians. Thus, the asymmetry of the conceptual background from which the parties to the conflict derived their arguments and upon which they based their actions becomes apparent.

> It would be incorrect to depict the conflict—which can be classified as a cultural or, more precisely, as a religious one—as proof of a clash of civilizations, or even of religions, carried out by "the masses." It was not entire religions or civilizations that found themselves on opposite sides of the conflict but, rather, a number of religiously inspired actors. Overall, the conflict can more readily be understood as what happens when fundamentalism comes in contact with dialogue-based conflict resolution.

It would be equally incorrect to label the dispute as prototypical of transnational religious conflict. In 1987, for example, German television personality Rudi Carrell caused a serious diplomatic incident by performing in a skit satirizing Iranian religious leader Ayatollah Khomeini. Likewise, almost two years later, following unrest in Pakistan, Khomeini issued a fatwa (i.e., an Islamic religious opinion) calling for the death of author Salman Rushdie, who lived in the United Kingdom. According to Iran's supreme leader, Rushdie had insulted Islam in his book *The Satanic Verses*. These examples show that reportage in Western media on Islamic issues had already been the cause of international crises. What was new in the case of the Mohammed cartoons was the almost simultaneous protests in a number of countries and the speed with which the parties to the conflict reacted to the reprinting of the cartoons and to the counter-protests.

At the same time, it seems unlikely that similar political conflicts will also reach crisis levels in the future. Germany's rapid establishment of an Islamic Conference following protests in 2006 targeting a Berlin production of Mozart's opera *Idomeneo*, for example, or efforts by well-regarded imams to defuse the situation following a speech given by Pope Benedict XVI in Regensburg, also in 2006, provide hope that such disputes will be solved differently in the future, with the various cultural contexts that frame the actors' actions being understood and addressed more quickly through conflict-resolution efforts. The mostly peaceful nature of the two conflicts mentioned above shows the appropriateness of this type of response.

Causes of Conflict and
the Significance of Cultural Context

The study summarized here by a number of its core findings is not only meant to deliver a theory-based conceptualization of "cultural conflicts" as a conflict type and to elucidate them by identifying them within the framework of recent conflicts, it also aims to examine their causes and to assess the efficacy of cultural values, such as language and religion, in analyzing global conflicts. The statistical processes used in the full-length version of this study (Croissant et al. 2009)[7] are taken from the standard set of tools used in quantitative social research. Since, however, the complete study evaluates explanatory variables that were only available through 2005 at the time of the analysis, the following observations are limited to this time period as well. This applies, above all, to economic variables, such as economic growth and average national per capita income.

Cultural factors and structures can relate to conflicts in two ways. First, they can help explain a conflict, that is, it can be assumed that cultural variables influence the probability that a conflict will take place. Such variables are referred to as explanatory factors (known as independent variables). Second, cultural conflicts can themselves be seen as the phenomenon needing explaining (known as dependent variables). Both cases are illustrated below.

---

7   Hypotheses were tested using binary logistic and linear regressions. Findings depicted here are based on binary logistic regressions, a procedure used for assessing the impact that multiple independent factors have on a variable, which, as in the case of the transformed CONIS data, is coded with two values (here: "1" for conflict, and "0" for no conflict).

Cultural fragmentation as conflict context

One possibility for assessing the cultural heterogeneity of various countries and comparing them across national borders is by using quantitative indicators to measure their linguistic and religious diversity. This study has thus developed three indices of cultural fragmentation:

– An index of linguistic fragmentation, which measures a country's linguistic diversity
– An index of religious fragmentation, which measures a country's religious diversity
– An index of cultural fragmentation, calculated as a composite of the first two indices and representing the degree of cultural (i.e., linguistic-religious) fragmentation present in a given country

For all three indicators, the higher the value, the greater the cultural fragmentation. To determine linguistic fragmentation, we have used the SIL Ethnologue dataset, which supplies a value for each country's linguistic heterogeneity in the form of Joseph Greenberg's diversity index. The Encyclopaedia Britannica yearbook 2007, in turn, served as the source for creating the religious fragmentation index, calculated using the same equation. Each country's cultural fragmentation was then derived from the arithmetic mean of its linguistic and religious indices.

The world map in Figure 10 shows each country's degree of linguistic fragmentation. For illustrative reasons, the countries have been divided into three groups, reflecting low, medium and high levels of fragmentation. Countries with little fragmentation have index values of between 0.00 and 0.29; countries with medium fragmentation have values of between 0.30 and 0.69; and countries with a high degree of fragmentation have values of between 0.70 and 1.00.

Clear regional differences are visible among countries in terms of their linguistic fragmentation. It becomes evident, for example, that countries located in the eastern Middle East—such as Oman, Iraq, Iran and Afghanistan—and in Central Asia and South Asia form a

Figure 10: Linguistic fragmentation worldwide

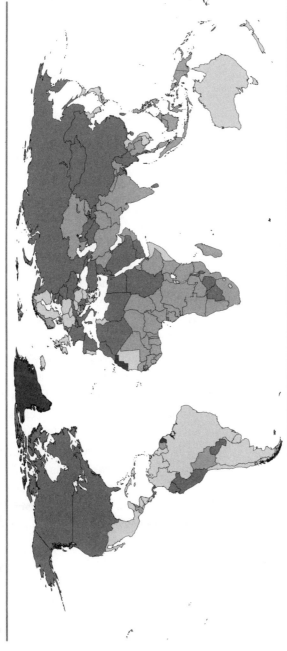

■ No data available   ☐ Little linguistic fragmentation   ■ Moderate linguistic fragmentation   ■ High linguistic fragmentation

Source: Authors' own analysis; depiction based on SIL International's 2005 "Ethnologue" (Gordon 2005).

geographic-cultural zone having a high degree of linguistic fragmentation. Similarly, sub-Saharan Africa is almost exclusively characterized by high levels of linguistic diversity.

Figure 11 (see inner back cover), which shows national religious characteristics around the globe, has been created in a similar fashion to depict each country's religious tendencies by illustrating to what degree the 16 religions tracked in this study are present among each nation's population.

If at least 30 percent of the population in a given country adheres to the most prevalent religion (i.e., the one having the greatest number of followers), that country is said to be "leaning towards" that religion. If at least 50 percent of the population adheres to the most prevalent religion, it is said to be "dominant." In turn, the most prevalent religion is said to be "hegemonic" if at least 80 percent of the population adheres to it. If at least 50 percent of the population adheres to one religion and at least 30 percent to another, or if two religions each account for at least 30 percent with neither reaching 50 percent, the country is considered asymmetrically or symmetrically "hybrid." If no religion is adhered to by at least 30 percent of the population, the country is considered religiously "fragmented."

Examining the globe's religious topography, a number of wide-ranging patterns become visible. The Christian world, for example, comprises primarily Europe, North and South America, Central and Southern Africa, Australia and New Zealand. The Islamic world stretches from North Africa southward to Western and Eastern Africa and also includes the entire Middle East and Pakistan as well as large parts of Central Asia. Christianity is also found in Pacific Asia, while Bangladesh and Indonesia, in particular, give Islam a significant Asian presence. The Buddhist world comprises primarily continental Southeast Asia as well as a number of South Asian countries, such as Bhutan and Sri Lanka. Hinduism predominates in India, and Japanese religions are found, of course, in Japan. Large numbers of atheists live, at least according to the background data, in China and North Korea. In terms of religious affiliation, hybrid states can be found on all continents, but especially in Africa and Eastern Europe.

In order to assess whether a correlation exists between linguistic and religious structures and the presence of conflict, the variables for linguistic, religious and cultural fragmentation were compared to each country's propensity for conflict. In order to track the possible impact of alternative explanatory factors, non-cultural variables were also used as control variables (multivariable analysis).

Multivariable analysis:
the relative explanatory power of cultural factors

The results of the multivariable analysis are presented below in two stages. First, the impact of cultural factors on all conflicts, in general, and cultural conflicts, in particular, is discussed. In addition, the findings are differentiated in terms of domestic and interstate conflicts and the dependent variables' various impacts. Second, a summary of the results for the control variables is presented, that is, for those non-cultural factors to which researchers ascribe, more or less justifiably, causality for the occurrence of political and, especially, cultural conflicts.

The impact of cultural variables on conflict (1950–2005)

Table 4 summarizes the findings of how cultural and non-cultural conflicts are influenced by cultural structures and characteristics. The point of departure is the assumption often encountered among researchers that a higher degree of cultural (i.e., religious or linguistic) heterogeneity results in a greater propensity for conflict. For illustrative purposes, a color scale and symbols are used to depict the level of causality. A plus sign (+) denotes a statistically positive correlation, and a minus sign (–) signals a statistically negative correlation, with a "0" representing an insignificant correlation.

Light gray is used to show those cases where higher levels of cultural fragmentation correlate significantly to a higher probability of

Table 4: How cultural variables impact domestic and
interstate conflicts (1950–2005)

	All Conflicts			
	Domestic Conflicts		**Interstate Conflicts**	
	(I) CONIS (3, 4, 5)*	**(II) CONIS (4, 5)****	**(III) CONIS (3, 4, 5)***	**(IV) CONIS (4, 5)****
Language	+	+	+	+
Religion	–	–	+	0
Culture (aggregated)	0	0	+	+

+ = positive coefficient at 5 % significance level; 0 = not significant; − = negative coefficient at 5 %
significance level. Based on the empirical findings in Croissant et al. (2009: 161 ff.).
Light gray signifies confirmation of the expected correlation; white signifies a lack of correlation;
and dark gray signifies findings that run counter to the expected correlation.

* = dichotomous dependent variable: CONIS conflict intensity at levels 1 and 2 = 0; levels 3, 4 and
5 = 1;
** = dichotomous dependent variable: CONIS conflict intensity at levels 1, 2 and 3 = 0; levels 4 and
5 = 1.

conflict. White is used to show those cases where no correlation was found. Dark gray shows those cases with a negative correlation, that is, where a high level of religious-linguistic, or cultural, fragmentation correlates to a low probability of conflict. The dark-gray fields represent instances that run counter to the presumed correlation.

The *findings for all (cultural and non-cultural) domestic conflicts* in columns I and II provide a differentiated picture of how cultural factors impact conflict. First, linguistic fragmentation seems to have the expected effect, in that a country's frequency of violence rises along with its degree of linguistic fragmentation. Second, counter to expectations, the index of religious fragmentation does not correlate positively to the level of conflict (cf. Croissant et al. 2009) since the probability of conflict falls in domestic contexts the more fragmented a country is in terms of the religions present there. Third and finally, the combined index of cultural fragmentation shows no correlation to domestic conflict. Evidently, the countervailing impacts of religious and linguistic fragmentation cancel each other out.

An examination of *how cultural factors impact interstate conflicts* (columns III and IV) shows that language and culture, in the form of the aggregate index, have a significant effect, as does religion, at least to some extent. That means that greater linguistic heterogeneity and cultural diversity increase a country's prospects of entering into violent conflict (cultural *and* non-cultural) with another nation-state. In terms of religious fragmentation, this same propensity for conflict can be seen when conflicts of all levels of intensity are considered. When comparing the indices' regression coefficients (not shown here), it becomes apparent that cultural fragmentation in its various guises plays a lesser role in interstate conflicts than in domestic conflicts. This is probably due to a number of causes, including the fact that conflict issues between states are usually different than those within a given country. In general, the approach used here has considerably greater power to explain domestic conflicts than interstate conflicts.

These findings refer to all violent conflicts and do not distinguish between cultural and non-cultural political conflicts. This study, however, has been carried out to examine cultural conflicts, which will thus be examined in detail. The relevant findings are summarized in Table 5. An *analysis of cultural conflicts at the domestic level* (columns V and VI) shows a pattern in part similar to the one found in Table 4 for all conflict types.

> The probability of a cultural conflict taking place increases significantly with the degree of linguistic fragmentation.

For example, level-3 cultural conflicts (violent crises) impact countries with a high degree of linguistic fragmentation twice as much as countries with only medium fragmentation, while, in the latter, cultural conflicts of level 4 or 5 intensity (limited and full-fledged warfare) have an impact that is three times as high as in countries that are linguistically fragmented only to a low degree.[8]

Table 5: How cultural variables impact domestic and interstate cultural conflicts (1950–2005)

	Cultural Conflicts			
	Domestic Cultural Conflicts		Interstate Cultural Conflicts	
	(V) CONIS (3, 4, 5)*	(VI) CONIS (4, 5)**	(VII) CONIS (3, 4, 5)*	(VIII) CONIS (4, 5)**
Language	+	+	+	+
Religion	–	0	–	–
Culture (aggregated)	+	+	+	+

+ = positive coefficient at 5 % significance level; 0 = not significant; – = negative coefficient at 5 % significance level. Based on the empirical findings in Croissant et al. (2009: 161 ff.).
Light gray signifies confirmation of the expected correlation; white signifies a lack of correlation; and dark gray signifies findings that run counter to the expected correlation.

* = dichotomous dependent variable: CONIS conflict intensity at levels 1 and 2 = 0; levels 3, 4 and 5 = 1;
** = dichotomous dependent variable: CONIS conflict intensity at levels 1, 2 and 3 = 0; levels 4 and 5 = 1.

> Such a linear relationship between fragmentation and conflict propensity is not evident in cases of religious diversity. Instead, the impact of cultural and non-cultural conflicts is at its highest level in countries that exhibit a medium level of religious fragmentation.

8 In countries with a low level of linguistic fragmentation, for example, the average impact of violent crisis is 0.06 (on a scale of 0 to 1), while the impact of highly violent conflicts is 0.04. In countries with medium linguistic fragmentation, these figures are, on average, 0.08 and 0.13, respectively, and in countries with a high degree of linguistic fragmentation, 0.17 and 0.22, respectively. More detailed information is available in Croissant et al. (2009).

This is particularly true of cultural disputes, in that a country with medium religious fragmentation is two and a half times more likely to experience high-intensity conflict than one that is relatively homogeneous in terms of the religions present there and even six times more likely to do so than countries that are especially heterogeneous in religious terms. Likewise, in the case of violent crises, countries with medium religious fragmentation are one and a half times more prone to violence than countries with low fragmentation and four times more prone than highly heterogeneous countries. In contrast to all conflicts, as depicted in Table 4, the combined index of cultural fragmentation proves highly significant for cultural conflicts, in that a higher level of combined linguistic-religious fragmentation leads to a higher propensity for conflict, regardless of whether all violent cultural conflicts are considered or only those with the highest intensity of violence.

In terms of *cultural conflicts between states* (columns VII and VIII), both linguistic and cultural fragmentation increase the likelihood of conflict, while religious fragmentation reduces it. In other words, a higher degree of linguistic and cultural diversity brings with it a higher probability of interstate conflict focusing on cultural issues, while religious fragmentation reduces this probability.

The findings on the correlation between religious fragmentation and the occurrence of cultural and non-cultural conflict both between and within countries need elucidation, given that they run counter to the standard presumption that higher levels of religious diversity result in higher levels of conflict, as expressed through popularized notions of Huntington's clash of civilizations as a "battle" between different religions. In addition to substantive explanations, that is, those illuminating the causality between religious factors and conflicts, other more mundane reasons can also be suggested, such as data quality and the systematic skewing that results when data are collected on religious structures within a given society.

The quality and reliability of the statistics on the religious characteristics of the countries examined here are indeed quite varied. While most industrialized countries have a range of detailed methods for collecting data, developing nations—which may or may not be venues for conflict in addition to all their other challenges—often have only rudimentary estimates at their disposal. Given the inaccuracy that results, it is plausible that more religious groups are accounted for in the more well-off industrialized countries (which tend to experience less conflict) than in developing nations. As a result, the index could produce results that are too low for developing nations by showing a lower level of fragmentation than is actually the case. In addition, it is feasible that certain religious communities might not be accounted for—that is, willfully ignored—in countries ruled by dictatorships (Alesina et al. 2003: 167).

The arguments above are predicated on the assumption that, as a country's cultural fragmentation rises, so does the number of its cultural actors and that this change is reflected in its cultural structures. As the number of actors increases, so does the probability of misunderstanding among actors, something that would ostensibly lead to a greater risk of conflict. This assumption of linear causality between cultural fragmentation and the risk of conflict (the more fragmented a society, the greater the probability of conflict) is, however, not necessarily plausible. While growing diversity does imply a greater number of actors, it is possible that this would not result in an increased risk of conflict. The prevailing assumption must therefore be further examined to see, for example, whether the connection between religious, linguistic and cultural fragmentation and the probability of conflict might, in fact, be non-linear.

Suggestions of such a non-linear relationship can, indeed, be found in the empirical literature (Ellingsen 2000; Collier and Hoeffler 1998, 2004; Rummel 1997; Fearon and Laitin 2003). Even if researchers advance disparate arguments, their studies converge around the thesis that the risk of conflict is not highest in highly fragmented (or homogenous) countries but, rather, in countries with medium levels of ethnic diversity—that is, those that are not too fragmented and not too homogenous (cf. Collier et al. 2003; Hegre et al. 2001). In terms of the degree of religious fragmentation, Reynal-Querol (2002), Fearon and Laitin (2003), Collier and Hoeffler (2004) and Montalvo and Reynal-Querol (2005) have ascertained that it has no impact on a society's risk of experiencing civil war (cf. De Juan and Hasenclever 2008).

Based on its findings, we believe our study does not confirm the scenario in which religious fragmentation has "no impact" on the risk of civil war. Instead, the probability of domestic conflict in countries with medium levels of fragmentation can be expected to increase not only as linguistic diversity does, but also along with religious diversity. In light of this, two empirical hypothesis were tested:

- Hypothesis 1: A medium degree of linguistic fragmentation increases the likelihood that a country will experience domestic conflict.
- Hypothesis 2: A medium degree of religious fragmentation increases the likelihood that a country will experience domestic conflict.[9]

The results show that, in the broader range of conflict, a medium level of linguistic fragmentation actually increases the probability of conflict, while in the narrower range (i.e., for more intensive conflicts), it has an attenuating affect. That means that level-3 conflicts, in particular, play a key role here. Yet, the opposite applies for the "interaction effect," that is, when medium-level linguistic diversity interacts with a sizeable youth bulge, in which case the probability of conflict rises.

An examination of countries with medium religious fragmentation also brings greater clarity to the findings. According to the findings, such countries are more often affected by conflict than those with lower or higher levels of religious diversity. Initial assumptions about religion are thus cast in a new light: Increasing religious diversity is not the core problem facing fragmented societies; rather, when a limited number of religious groups of roughly equivalent size is present, the probability of conflict rises, for all conflicts, in general, and for cultural conflicts, in particular.

---

9 For testing purposes, a dummy variable was employed. Countries with a medium level of religious and linguistic fragmentation—that is, fragmentation variables with values between 0.3 and 0.7 (with both types of fragmentation measured on a scale between 0 and 1)—were assigned a value of 1. If the indicator value was less than 0.3 or greater than 0.7, the dummy variable was assigned a value of 0.

In sum, three key findings present themselves across all categories and analyses:

- A country's linguistic fragmentation directly increases the probability that a conflict will arise, both in the domestic and the interstate context (including cultural conflicts).
- The combined index of cultural fragmentation also promotes conflict to a large extent.
- The study's findings suggest a non-linear relationship between religious fragmentation and the propensity for conflict, in that countries that are either highly fragmented or particularly homogenous seem to be less impacted by conflict than countries with a medium level of religious diversity.

Countervailing influences

Consensus exists among specialists working in the field of conflict and war research that political and violent conflicts cannot be traced back solely to individual causative factors. This is, of course, also true for cultural factors. Although our study provides evidence that certain cultural factors can positively or negatively influence the probability of conflict—that is, can promote or hinder conflict—religious, cultural and, especially, linguistic fragmentation are factors that, as independent variables, can affect the probability of conflict, that is, the dependent variable. Yet they are presumably not the only factors that influence the occurrence of cultural and non-cultural conflicts. In addition, it might plausibly be assumed that cultural variables interact with other non-cultural factors and that they either reinforce or mitigate each other. The validity of this assumption is examined below.

The research literature, in fact, offers a comprehensive range of explanatory variables that go beyond cultural structures and influences. It is not possible to assess here the derivation of these variables or approaches. It must be noted, instead, that the current study's findings are based on a logistic regression model that contains a number of standard factors for explaining the probability of conflict in addition to cultural context, on the one hand, and that simultaneously checks for countervailing causalities among these factors, on the other (cf. Croissant et al. 2009).

In deploying these "control variables," the basic model focuses on comparative studies taken from the research literature (Fearon and Laitin 2003; Collier and Hoeffler 2004; Hegre and Sambanis 2006). The variables in use account for a country's level of development and democratization as well as its social fragmentation, international economic interdependence, arable land mass, level of migration and migration flows, and economic growth—in other words, those explanatory factors that are generally considered relevant in quantitative empirical conflict research (cf. Croissant et al. 2009).

This standard model has been augmented by an additional variable that can be seen as a significant challenge to hypotheses focusing on culture: the youth bulge (Huntington 1997; Heinsohn 2003; Urdal 2004, 2006). The youth bulge is measured as the number of males between the ages of 15 and 24 as a percentage of the overall male population at least 15 years of age. Of these control variables, a number have proven meaningful for explaining the domestic and interstate conflicts under study. Their impacts are as follows:

- Population size directly increases the probability of conflict.
- The percentage of young males between the ages of 15 and 24 (the youth bulge) directly increases the probability of conflict.
- Infant mortality (used to gauge a country's underdevelopment) increases the likelihood of conflict, especially in the domestic context.
- A high level of economic growth reduces the likelihood of conflict, especially in the domestic context.
- The greater the amount of arable land available, the lower the probability that conflict will occur.
- Countries with more-developed democracies are less likely to experience conflict.

The degree to which a country is integrated into the global economy is irrelevant for all types of conflict examined here, although this finding is at odds with the adage that "those who trade don't wage war." What's more, the findings for migration flows are dichotomous: In the case of domestic conflicts (both for cultural conflicts, in particular, and all conflicts, in general) immigrant inflows diminish the likelihood of conflict, while inflows increase the probability of conflict in the interstate context.

The youth bulge as a challenge to the "clash of civilizations" theory

The findings are remarkable, moreover, since they confirm the youth bulge as a new explanatory factor that—in addition to cultural fragmentation and, possibly, in interaction with it—increases the risk of conflict. The youth bulge theory is predicated on an examination of age structures within the population pyramid, that is, not the pyramid's size but, rather, its form. The assumption is that the relative size of the young-male demographic —a group especially focused on acquiring status—plays a key role in determining the risk of conflict in a given society (Heinsohn 2003). In contrast to Malthusian approaches,[10] the population is not treated in an undifferentiated manner (Fuller and Pitts 1990: 20); rather, the size of one specific age group is examined along with its impact on the rest of society.

Conflict scenarios predicated on a youth bulge have existed for quite some time. For example, Goldstone (1991) explains the English civil war in the 17th century by noting the growing share of young men within the population. Moller (1968) traces the role young males have played in social upheavals from the Reformation and French Revolution to the race riots in the United States in the 1960s. He argues, for example, that National Socialism's rise was due to the global

10 Thomas Robert Malthus (1766–1834) was concerned with the problems that arise from a constantly growing population and limited resources. In his investigations, he considered the human population as uniform and did not differentiate between population groups with individual needs and behaviors.

economic crisis impacting what was an exceptionally young population (Moller 1968: 243 ff.). These examples make clear that conflicts
that can, in part, be "construed" as cultural conflicts might, in fact,
be fueled by demographic developments (namely, a youth bulge),
while differences between religious, linguistic or cultural groups or
ideologies are solely the catalysts that ignite the disputes.

In terms of contemporary events, Gary Fuller (1995; Fuller and
Pitts 1990) has, in particular, examined youth bulges in Asia. He
reaches the conclusion that the size of the youth bulge relates directly
to the occurrence and intensity of conflict. His thesis gained promi-
nence, above all, as a result of Huntington (1997), who used youth
bulges to underpin his "clash of civilizations" theory (Huntington
1997: 156, 174). Huntington thus explains the high rate of participation of Muslim countries in wars occurring along intercultural fault
lines and the increase of Islamist movements and violence as resulting from the critical pressures that arise from massive population increases: "The demographic explosion in Muslim societies and the
availability of large numbers of often unemployed males between the
ages of 15 and 30 is a natural source of instability and violence both
within Islam and against non-Muslims. Whatever other causes may
be at work, this factor alone would go a long way to explaining Muslim violence in the 1980s and 1990s" (ibid.: 433).

It must be critically noted that the simple formula of "share of
young males = violence and conflict" is too short-sighted (cf. Heinsohn 2003: 24, 55). More decisive are the ancillary conditions that can
ignite the potential for violence that results when a youth bulge is present. Against this background, demographic criteria cannot be seen as
wholly deterministic, as is sometimes argued (Fuller and Pitts 1990: 13).

Figure 12 shows the global distribution of the number of 15-
to 24-year-old males as a percentage of the overall population at least
15 years old. With the exception of Turkey and Mexico, this age group
represents less than 22 percent of all adults in OECD member states.
The highest concentration can be found in sub-Saharan Africa as well
as in the Middle East and Central Asia, including Pakistan, where (in
most countries) more than one-third of all adults are under 25 years

Figure 12: Male youth bulge, 2005

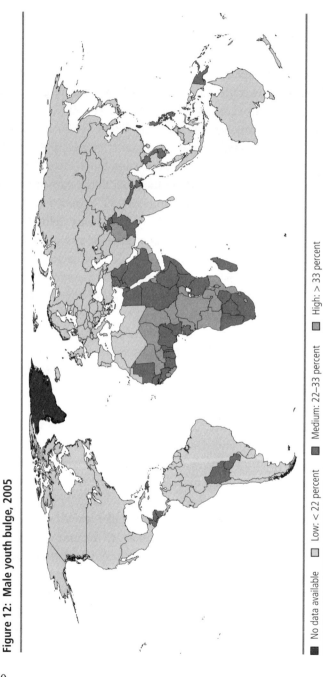

■ No data available   ☐ Low: < 22 percent   ■ Medium: 22–33 percent   ■ High: > 33 percent

The illustration depicts the youth bulge, which measures the number of male 15- to 24-year-olds as a percentage of the general population at least 15 years of age.

Source: Authors' own analysis based on UNWPP (United Nations 2005)

of age. The global leader, at 47.2 percent, is Swaziland, a country where almost half of all adults are younger than 25 years of age. The lowest share can be found in Italy, at 12.6 percent.

If one examines the relationship between the occurrence of youth bulges and conflicts, one finds a moderate-to-strong statistical correlation for all key international conflict indicators. In other words, the higher the surplus of young men, the more conflicts that take place— a fact, however, that cannot be reduced to the overly simplified formula noted above of "share of young males = violence and conflict" since no automatic causality is apparent (cf. Wagschal, Metz and Schwank 2008). At the same time, the CONIS data confirm this moderately strong correlation between the male youth bulge and the level of conflict, as can be seen in Figure 13.

Interdependency and non-linearity of explanatory factors

The direct correlation in Figure 13 gives rise to the presumption that a youth bulge can influence the level of conflict a country experiences. Yet it remains questionable whether the impact of a (male) youth bulge remains significant within a multivariable analysis that also takes other theoretically plausible factors into account. Empiric tests were carried out to this end in the full-length version of the study documented here. The findings show that population is an important factor relating to conflict frequency, in that a large share of young males noticeably increases the probability of conflict. In general, this supports the theory that a youth bulge, often overlooked until now, plays a key role in explaining the likelihood of conflict occurring within a given country.

Theoretically, however, it is also plausible that cultural factors and youth bulges interact, giving rise to the question of whether the various variables measuring cultural fragmentation do so as well. Such an interaction between linguistic fragmentation and the youth bulge was examined in the domestic context. The results reveal that both factors do, in fact, interact in the most violent disputes (levels 4 and 5) to increase the likelihood of conflict.

Figure 13: Conflict intensity and male youth bulge*

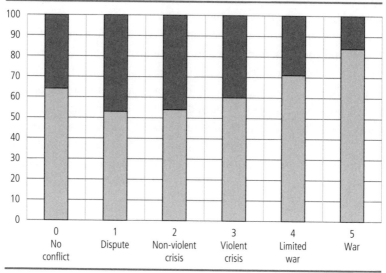

All data = Percentages within individual subgroups

* Number of 15- to 24-year-olds as share of total population at least 15 years old

The various conflict levels were broken into two groups: Lower level conflicts from 0 to 3 were assigned a value of "0," while the categories of limited warfare and war (conflict levels 4 and 5) were assigned a value of "1." The figure depicts the relative frequency of the country-years within the individual levels of conflict with above-average (light gray) and below-average (dark gray) youth bulges.

Source: Authors' own analysis based on the CONIS database

As a final finding, the following must be noted: The interactive effect between cultural and demographic factors (linguistic fragmentation and youth bulge) is particularly pronounced in cultural conflicts. In cases where a high degree of linguistic fragmentation coexists with a large youth bulge, the probability increases that highly violent cultural conflicts, in particular, will occur.

Across a broader scale (intensity levels 3, 4 and 5), however, a negative correlation can be seen, that is, the interaction of linguistic fragmentation and youth bulge reduces the likelihood that (cultural) conflicts will take place.

Conclusion

Looking at the cultural dimensions of global conflicts from 1945 to 2007, this study considers "cultural conflicts" from two vantage points. First, they are examined as a "dependent" variable (i.e., as a phenomenon to be explained). Second, cultural factors are investigated as causal agents (i.e., as "independent" variables). Cultural conflicts are thus defined as political conflicts that focus on language, religion or historical contexts. In cultural conflicts, culture is not necessarily the cause of a conflict but, rather, the issue around which it revolves.

The analysis shows that cultural conflicts are clearly a domestic phenomenon, with more than four out of five such conflicts taking place within national borders.

The pattern of such conflicts has changed over time as well. Since 1945, the share of cultural conflicts as a percentage of total global conflicts has been considerable, with the absolute number surpassing the number of non-cultural conflicts for the first time in the mid-1980s. Indeed, in 2007, there were more cultural conflicts than ever before.

Religious and, in particular, historicitary conflicts predominate among cultural conflicts in both the domestic and interstate context, and the end of the Cold War represents a caesura in how cultural conflicts have evolved, especially when it comes to domestic conflicts. Since then, the number of religious and historicitary conflicts has increased dramatically.

In terms of the level of violence, differences exist among the various types of conflict as well, with cultural conflicts particularly prone to violence, in that the share of cultural conflicts rises along with the intensity of the strife in both domestic and international settings.

Regional differences are also clearly visible, above all in the domestic context. Religious conflicts are typical of the Middle East, while, in Asia, historicitary conflicts tend to predominate, and Europe tends to be a venue for linguistic conflicts. Africa, in turn, shows ambivalent patterns when it comes to cultural and non-cultural conflicts, while the Americas are clearly home to non-cultural conflicts.

The study's quantitative analysis shows, moreover, that the probability of domestic cultural conflict and of all types of interstate conflict increases the higher a country's cultural and, in particular, linguistic fragmentation.

If one looks at the relevance of conflict causes, language plays a key role and is more significant than religious fragmentation, in that the degree of linguistic fragmentation most readily increases the probability of conflicts both within and between states.

It can also be seen that, in addition to cultural variables, other factors influence the likelihood of conflict taking place. Cultural variables can therefore not be seen as "master variables" since conflicts are also more likely to ensue the greater a country's population, the higher the share of young men it is home to, the less arable land it has at its disposal and the lower its economic growth. In contrast to the assumption that a direct causality exists between religious fragmentation and the likelihood of conflict, a much more compelling explanation for domestic conflicts is the interaction of medium levels of religious fragmentation with demographic factors, such as a youth bulge (i.e., a large number of young males as a percentage of the overall population).

Overall, cultural structures are significant factors in explaining conflicts. A more telling factor, however, is a non-cultural phenomenon—the youth bulge—especially when it interacts with cultural factors. Ultimately, evidence exists to suggest a non-linear relationship between cultural factors and conflicts. Countries with a moderate level of linguistic and religious fragmentation exhibit a higher probability of conflict, which in turn is reinforced by the presence of a greater share of young men within the general population (i.e., a youth bulge).

In the present study, theories relating to cultural conflict were examined empirically by using a comprehensive dataset to cast the often very emotional debate on how the globe's cultures interact in a new light. The results show that cultural conflicts have not taken place only following the Cold War but, instead, have had a significant presence during the entire period under observation. Although cultural conflicts have increased in frequency during the observation period, this does not necessarily mean that the world's cultures are having greater difficulty coexisting.

Instead, technological advances, increasing opportunities for travel and greater prosperity have made numerous new contacts between cultures possible and multiplied the risk of violence ensuing from misunderstandings and intolerance. Accordingly, when one considers the innumerable contacts and massive communication that take place among the world's cultures and the resulting potential for conflict, the number of actual violent conflicts is actually miniscule.

This study cannot, of course, answer all the questions relating to this topic. It has been able to show, however, that certain issues, such as historical experiences relating to cultural coexistence, lead more often to escalation and that certain external conditions have an ameliorating or aggravating effect. Further research will be needed to determine how culture, as a factor promoting conflict, relates to the power of intercultural dialogue to promote peace. In terms of a rapidly changing world's propensity for cultural conflict, additional research will also need to examine where current dangers exist and where new flashpoints are forming.

One critical point must be remembered: The findings show that cultural conflict does not automatically lead to violence, that is, that no sole imaginable cultural profile exists for any given society that inevitably gives rise to conflict and violence. Conversely, all of the conflicts in which violence has been terminated make clear that social groups and other actors can learn to coexist without violence, even if the speed of this learning process varies. Success factors here include the basic principles of intercultural dialogue: an appreciation of diversity, a recognition of the other side's equality and intercultural competence on the part of the participating actors. These factors create the framework in which all parties can communicate peacefully as they examine cultural differences, the difficulties that result from such differences and the possibilities for identifying a canon of common values.

References

Afigbo, Adiele. The National Question in Nigerian History, Politics and Affairs. In *Nigerian History, Politics and Affairs. The Collected Essays of Adiele Afigbo*, edited by Toyin Falola. Trenton 2005: 405–420.

Ahanotu, Austin Metumara. *Religion, State and Society in Contemporary Africa. Nigeria, Sudan, South Africa, Zaire and Mozambique.* New York 1992.

Akinwumi, Olayemi. *Crises and Conflicts in Nigeria. A Political History Since 1960.* Münster 2004.

Alesina, Alberto, Arnaud Devleeschauwer, William Easterly, Sergio Kurlat and Romain Wacziarg. Fractionalization. *Journal of Economic Growth* (8) 2: 155–194, 2003.

Aspinall, Edward. The Construction of Grievance. National resources and identity in a separatist conflict. *Journal of Conflict Resolution* (51) 6: 950–972, 2007.

Berger, Alois. "Zwei Belgien in einem. Das schwierige Verhältnis zwischen Flamen und Wallonen". *Deutschlandfunk.* Broadcast Dec. 17, 2005.

Bertrand, Jacques. Democratization and Religious and Nationalist Conflict in Post-Suharto Indonesia. In *Democratization and Identity: Regimes and Ethnicity in East and Southeast Asia*, edited by Susan Henders. Lanham 2004a: 177–201.

Bertrand, Jacques. *Nationalism and Ethnic Conflict in Indonesia.* Cambridge 2004b.

Billington, Rosamund, Sheelagh Strawbridge, Lenore Greensides and Annette Fitzsimons. *Culture and Society: A Sociology of Culture.* Houndmills 1991.

Boecker, Malte. Impacts of rapid social change in South East Asia: introduction. *Asien* (110) January: 9–12, 2009.

Bonacker, Thorsten. *Kommunikation zwischen Konsens und Konflikt. Möglichkeiten und Grenzen gesellschaftlicher Rationalität bei Jürgen Habermas und Niklas Luhmann.* Oldenburg 1997.

Bonacker, Thorsten (ed.). *Sozialwissenschaftliche Konflikttheorien. Eine Einführung.* Wiesbaden 2008.

Bonacker, Thorsten, and Andreas Reckwitz (eds.). *Kulturen der Moderne. Soziologische Perspektiven der Gegenwart.* Frankfurt am Main 2007.

Brown, Graham. Horizontal Inequalities, Ethnic Separatism and Violent Conflict. The Case of Aceh, Indonesia. *Human Development Report Office Occasional Paper 2005/28.*

"Brutale Gewalt. Kampf der Kulturen nach Satire". *NDR. ZAPP. Das Medienmagazin.* Feb. 8, 2006. (Also available online at www3.ndr.de/ndrtv_pages_std/0,3147,OID2284542_REF2488,00.html, accessed Oct. 31, 2008.)

Chardon, Matthias. Belgien nach der Parlamentswahl. Nach innen instabil, nach außen verlässlicher EU-Partner? Europäische Identität wichtig für Belgien. 2007. www.cap-lmu.de/aktuell/positionen/2007/belgien.php (accessed April 24, 2008).

Chojnacki, Sven. *Dyadische Konflikte und die Eskalation zum Krieg. Prozesse und Strukturbedingungen dyadischer Gewalt in Europa, 1816–1992.* Berlin 1999.

Chojnacki, Sven. *Wandel der Gewaltformen im internationalen System, 1946–2006.* Osnabrück 2008.

Chukwuma, Michael. *Nigerian Politics and the Role of Religion: An Analysis of the Role of Religion in Nigerian Politics at the Early Stages of National Integration.* Bonn 1985.

Collier, Paul, and Anke Hoeffler. On economic causes of civil war. *Oxford Economic Papers* (50) 4: 563–573, 1998.

Collier, Paul, and Anke Hoeffler. Greed and grievance in civil war. *Oxford Economic Papers* (56) 4: 563–596, 2004.

Collier, Paul, Lani Elliott, Håvard Hegre, Marta Reynal-Querol and Nicholas Sambanis. *Breaking the Conflict Trap.* Washington 2003.

Croissant, Aurel, and Christoph Trinn. Culture, identity and conflict in Asia and Southeast Asia. *Asien* (110) January: 13–43, 2009.

Croissant, Aurel, Uwe Wagschal, Nicolas Schwank and Christoph Trinn. *Die kulturellen Dimensionen des globalen Konfliktgeschehens. Kulturelle Konflikte seit 1945.* Baden-Baden 2009.

De Coorebyter, Vincent. "Zwei- bis dreifaches Belgien. Flandern, Wallonien und Brüssel finden keinen gemeinsamen Nenner". *Le Monde diplomatique.* Nov. 9, 2007. 6–7. (www.monde-diplomatique.de/pm/2007/11/09.mondeText.artikel.a0036.idx.10/.)

De Juan, Alexander, and Andreas Hasenclever. Framing religious conflicts. Die Rolle von Eliten in religiös konnotierten Gewaltkonflikten. Conference paper presented at "Identität, Institutionen und Ökonomie: Ursachen innenpolitischer Gewalt," Feb. 22–23, 2008, Constance.

De Winter, Lieven, and Patrick Dumont. Do Belgian parties undermine the democratic chain of delegation? *West European Politics* (29) 5: 957–978, 2006.

De Winter, Lieven, Marc Swyngedouw and Patrick Dumont. Party system(s) and electoral behaviour in Belgium. From stability to balkanisation. *West European Politics* (29) 5: 933–956, 2006.

Diamond, Larry. *Class, Ethnicity and Democracy in Nigeria: The Failure of the First Republic.* Houndsmill 1988.

Dörner, Andreas. Politische Kulturforschung. In *Politikwissenschaft. Ein Grundkurs,* edited by Herfried Münkler. Reinbek 2003: 587–619.

Dumont, Patrick, and Jean-François Caulier. The "Effective Number of Relevant Parties". How Voting Power Improves Laakso-Taagepera's Index. *CEREC Working Paper* Dec. 11, 2003. http://centres.fusl.ac.be/CEREC/document/2003/cerec2003_7.pdf (accessed July 22, 2007).

Eller, Jack. *From Culture to Ethnicity to Conflict: An Anthropological Perspective on International Ethnic Conflict.* Ann Arbor 1999.

Ellingsen, Tanja. Colorful community or ethnic witches' brew? Multiethnicity and domestic conflict during and after the Cold War. *Journal of Conflict Resolution* (44) 2: 228–249, 2000.

Encyclopaedia Britannica. *Britannica Book of the Year.* Chicago 2007.

Esposito, John. *Islam: The Straight Path.* New York 1988.

Esser, Hartmut. *Soziologie. Spezielle Grundlagen; Band 1: Situationslogik und Handeln.* Frankfurt am Main 1999.

Falter, Rolf. Belgium's Peculiar Way to Federalism. In *Nationalism in Belgium. Shifting Identities 1780–1995,* edited by Kas Depres and Louis Vos. London 1998: 177–197.

Fearon, James, and David Laitin. Ethnicity, insurgency, and civil war. *American Political Science Review* (97) 1: 75–90, 2003.

Fleischer, Michael. *Kulturtheorie. Systemtheoretische und evolutionäre Grundlagen.* Oberhausen 2001.

Fukuyama, Francis. *Das Ende der Geschichte. Wo stehen wir?* Munich 1992.

Fuller, Gary. The Demographic Backdrop to Ethnic Conflict. A Geographic Overview. In *The Challenge of Ethnic Conflict to National and International Order in the 1990s. Geographic Perspectives. A conference report,* edited by Central Intelligence Agency. Washington, D.C. 1995: 95–139.

Fuller, Gary, and Forrest Pitts. Youth cohorts and political unrest in South Korea. *Political Geography Quarterly* (9) 1: 9–22, 1990.

Geertz, Clifford. *Dichte Beschreibung. Beiträge zum Verstehen kultureller Systeme.* Frankfurt am Main 1994.

Gleason, Philip. Identifying identity. A semantic history. *The Journal of American History* (69) 4: 910–931, 1983.

Goffman, Erving. *Rahmen-Analyse. Ein Versuch über die Organisation von Alltagserfahrungen.* Frankfurt am Main 1977.

Goldstone, Jack. *Revolution and Rebellion in the Early Modern World.* Berkeley 1991.

Gordon, Raymond. Ethnologue. Languages of the World. 2005. www.ethnologue.com/ethno_docs/distribution.asp?by=country (accessed July 22, 2007).

Gurr, Ted. *Why Men Rebel.* Princeton 1970.

Hadiwinata, Bob Sugeng. From Violence to Voting. Post-Conflict Settlement and Democratization in Aceh. Unpublished manuscript 2006.

Hamid, Ahmad Fauzi Abdul. Repoliticisation of Islam in Southeast Asia. *Asien* (110) January: 44–67, 2009.

Hansen, Klaus. *Kultur und Kulturwissenschaft. Eine Einführung.* Tübingen 2000.

Harbom, Lotta, and Peter Wallensteen. Armed conflict: 1989–2006. *Journal of Peace Research* (44) 5: 623–634, 2007.

Harnischfeger, Johannes. *Demokratisierung und islamisches Recht. Der Scharia-Konflikt in Nigeria.* Frankfurt am Main 2006.

Hasenclever, Andreas, Klaus-Dieter Wolf and Michael Zürn (eds.). *Macht und Ohnmacht internationaler Institutionen.* Frankfurt am Main 2007.

Hasenclever, Andreas, and Volker Rittberger. *The Impact of Faith: Does Religion Make a Difference in Political Conflict?* Tübingen 1999.

Hecking, Claus. *Das politische Systems Belgiens.* Opladen 2003.

Hegre, Håvard, and Nicholas Sambanis. Sensitivity analysis of empirical results on civil war onset. *Journal of Conflict Resolution* (50) 4: 508–535, 2006.

Hegre, Håvard, Tanja Ellingsen, Scott Gates and Nils Gleditsch. Toward a democratic civil peace? Democracy, political change and civil war, 1816–1992. *American Political Science Review* (95) 1: 33–48, 2001.

Heinsohn, Gunnar. *Söhne und Weltmacht. Terror im Aufstieg und Fall der Nationen.* Zurich 2003.

Horowitz, Donald. *Ethnic Groups in Conflict.* Berkeley 1985.

Huntington, Samuel. The clash of civilizations? *Foreign Affairs* (72) 3: 22–49, 1993.

Huntington, Samuel. *Kampf der Kulturen. Die Neugestaltung der Weltpolitik im 21. Jahrhundert.* Munich 1997.

Krallmann, Dieter, and Andreas Ziemann. *Grundkurs Kommunikationswissenschaft.* Munich 2001.

Luhmann, Niklas. *Soziale Systeme. Grundriß einer allgemeinen Theorie.* Frankfurt am Main 1984.

Luhmann, Niklas. *Soziale Systeme. Grundriß einer allgemeinen Theorie.* Frankfurt am Main 1985.

McCarthy, John. The demonstration effect. Natural resources, ethno-nationalism and the Aceh conflict. *Singapore Journal of Tropical Geography* (28) 3: 314–333, 2007.

McCulloch, Lesley. Greed: The Silent Force of Conflict in Aceh. In *Violence in Between. Conflict and Security in Archipelagic Southeast Asia*, edited by Damien Kingsbury. Singapore 2005: 203–231.

Missbach, Antje. Aceh's Guerillas: The Internal Transformation of Gerakan Aceh Merdeka (GAM). In *Democratization in Indonesia: After the Fall of Suharto*, edited by Ingrid Wessel. Berlin 2005: 163–171.

Moller, Herbert. Youth as a force in the modern world. *Comparative studies in society and history* (10) 3: 237–260, 1968.

Montalvo, José, and Marta Reynal-Querol. Ethnic polarization, potential conflict, and civil wars. *American Economic Review* (95) 3: 796–816, 2005.

Müller-Thederan, Dirk. "Staatskrise. Königreich Belgien steht vor der Spaltung". *Welt Online*. Nov. 9, 2007. (Also available online at www.welt.de/politik.article1345615/Koenigreich_Belgien_steht_vor_der_Spaltung.html, accessed April 24, 2008.)

Okafor, Gabriel Maduka. *Development of Christianity and Islam in Modern Nigeria*. Würzburg 1992.

Parsons, Talcott. A Paradigm of the Human Condition. In *Action Theory and the Human Condition*, edited by Talcott Parsons. New York 1978: 352–433.

Pelinka, Anton. Religion und Politik. Versuch einer systemischen Analyse. In *Recht—Politik—Wirtschaft. Dynamische Perspektiven*, edited by Konrad Arnold, Friederike Bundschuh-Rieseneder, Arno Kahl, Thomas Müller and Klaus Wallnöfer. Vienna 2008: 461–475.

Proissl, Wolfgang. "Belgien ist unregierbar". *Financial Times Deutschland*. Dec. 2, 2007. (Also available online at www.ftd.de/politik.europa/:Belgien/287017.html, accessed April 24, 2008.)

"Radikale Muslime bedrohen Europäer". *Süddeutsche.de*. Feb. 3, 2006. (Also available online at www.sueddeutsche.de/politik/423/3582 49/text/, accessed April 4, 2008.)

Rae, Douglas, and Michael Taylor. *The Analysis of Political Cleavages*. New Haven 1970.

Ramelsberger, Annette, and Manuela Kessler. "Wütende Muslime schwören 'heiligen Krieg.'" *Sueddeutsche.de*. Feb. 3, 2006. (Also available online at www.sueddeutsche.de/politik/863/354693/text/, accessed April 4, 2008.)

Reimann, Anna, "Dänische Zeitungen drucken Karikaturen nach". *Spiegel Online*. Feb. 13, 2008. (Also available online at www.spiegel.de/politik/ausland/0,1518,534942,00.html, accessed April 4, 2008).

Reynal-Querol, Marta. Ethnicity, political systems and civil wars. *Journal of Conflict Resolution* (46) 1: 29–54, 2002.

Rochtus, Dirk. Die belgische "Nationalitätsfrage" als Herausforderung für Europa. *Discussions Paper Zentrum für Europäische Integrationsforschung*. 1998. www.zeit.de/download/zeit_dp/dp_c27_rochtus.pdf (accessed April 24, 2008).

Ross, Michael. Resources and Rebellion in Aceh, Indonesia. In *Understanding Civil Wars. Evidence and Analysis, Volume 2*, edited by Paul Collier and Nicholas Sambanis. Washington, D.C. 2005: 35–69.

Rummel, Rudolph. Is collective violence correlated with social pluralism? *Journal of Peace Research* (34) 2: 163–175, 1997.

Sarkees, Meredith. The correlates of war data on war. An update to 1997. *Conflict Management and Peace Science* (18) 1: 123–144, 2000.

"Saudis recall envoy in Danish row". *BBC Online*. Jan. 26, 2006. (Also available online at http://news.bbc.co.uk/2/hi/europe/4651714.stm, accessed April 4, 2008.)

Schlötzer, Christiane. "Ein Sturm der Entrüstung, gezielt entfesselt". *Sueddeutsche.de*. Feb. 3, 2006. (Also available online at www.sueddeutsche.de/politik/655/362477/text/, accessed April 4, 2008.)

Schulze, Kirsten. *The Free Aceh Movement (GAM): Anatomy of a Separatist Organization*. Washington, D.C. 2004.

Schulze, Kirsten. Insurgency and Counter-Insurgency: Strategy and the Aceh Conflict, October 1976–May 2004. In *Verandah of Violence: Aceh's Contested Place in Indonesia*, edited by Anthony Reid. Singapore 2006: 225–271.

Schwank, Nicolas. *Konflikte, Krisen, Kriege. Merkmale und Dynamiken internationaler politischer Konflikte 1945–2005*. Baden-Baden (in print).

Searle, Peter. Ethno-religious conflicts: Rise or decline? *Contemporary Southeast Asia* (24) 1: 1–12, 2002.

Senghaas, Dieter. *Gewalt – Konflikt – Frieden. Essays zur Friedensforschung.* Hamburg 1974.

Senghaas, Dieter. *Zivilisierung wider Willen. Der Konflikt der Kulturen mit sich selbst.* Frankfurt am Main 1998.

Senghaas, Dieter. *Zum irdischen Frieden. Erkenntnisse und Vermutungen.* Frankfurt am Main 2004.

Seul, Jeffrey. "Ours is the way of god": Religion, identity and intergroup conflict. *Journal of Peace Research* (36) 5: 553–569, 1999.

Severino, Rodolfo C. Regional economic integration and cultural change. *Asien* (110) January: 68–72, 2009.

Sherlock, Stephen. The Tyranny of Invented Traditions: Aceh. In *Violence in Between: Conflict and Security in Archipelagic Southeast Asia*, edited by Damien Kingsbury. Singapore 2005: 175–203.

Singer, David, and Melvin Small. *The Wages of War 1816–1965: A Statistical Handbook.* New York 1972.

Small, Melvin, and David Singer. *Resort to Arms. International and Civil Wars, 1816–1980.* Beverly Hills 1982.

Smelser, Neil. Culture: Coherent or Incoherent. In *Theory of Culture*, edited by Richard Münch and Neil Smelser. Berkeley 1992: 3–28.

Strikwerda, Carl. *A House Divided: Catholics, Socialists and Flemish Nationalists in Nineteenth-Century Belgium.* Oxford 1997.

Swenden, Wilfried, Marleen Brans and Lieven De Winter. The politics of Belgium: Institutions and policy under bipolar and centrifugal federalism. *West European Politics* (29) 5: 836–876, 2006.

Thayer, Carlyle A. Multilateral cooperation and building trust: Ideas for EU-Asian relations. *Asien* (110) January: 73–97, 2009.

Trompenaars, Fons, and Charles Hampden-Turner. *Riding the Waves of Culture. Understanding Cultural Diversity in Business.* London 2002.

United Nations. *World Population Prospects. The 2004 Revision. Extended dataset.* New York 2005.

Urdal, Henrik. The devil in the demographics. The effect of youth bulges on domestic armed conflict, 1950–2000. *The World Bank, Social Development Working Paper* 14 2004.

Urdal, Henrik. A clash of generations? Youth bulges and political violence. *International Studies Quarterly* (50) 3: 607–629, 2006.

Wagschal, Uwe, Thomas Metz and Nicolas Schwank. Ein "demografischer Frieden"? Der Einfluss von Bevölkerungsfaktoren auf inner- und zwischenstaatliche Konflikte. *Zeitschrift für Politikwissenschaft* (18) 3: 353–383, 2008.

Wallensteen, Peter, and Margareta Sollenberg. Armed conflict 1989–2000. *Journal of Peace Research* (38) 5: 629–644, 2001.

Weber, Max. Die "Objektivität" sozialwissenschaftlicher und sozialpolitischer Erkenntnis. In *Gesammelte Aufsätze zur Wissenschaftslehre,* edited by Johannes Winckelmann. Tübingen 1988: 146–214.

Weingardt, Markus A. *Religion Macht Frieden. Das Friedenspotential von Religionen in politischen Gewaltkonflikten.* Stuttgart 2007.

"Wie es zum Karikaturen-Streit gekommen ist. Chronologie einer gesteuerten Eskalation in der muslimischen Welt". *NZZ Online.* Feb. 20, 2006. (Also available online at www.nzz.ch/2006/02/20/al/articleDLH7M.html, accessed Oct. 31, 2008.)